Praise for
THIS BOOK IS CHEAPER THAN THERAPY

"*This Book Is Cheaper Than Therapy* is an amazing resource for anyone looking to improve their mental and emotional health. Liz Kelly has created a fun, accessible, and highly practical guide that spans a wide range of key topics yet is also thoroughly backed by science. And it doesn't hurt that it's a genuinely funny book, too, which will keep you wanting more! This book is a must-read!"

—**Jonah Paquette**, clinical psychologist and author of *Happily Even After*

"A no-fluff and no-clichés framework that will see you enhance your emotional resilience, cultivate meaningful relationships, and get clear on exactly how to build a life that you don't want to run away from. *This Book Is Cheaper Than Therapy* will have you laughing as much as you've been crying, as Liz Kelly very quickly becomes not only your therapist but your hilarious and relatable best friend! A must-read if you're looking to take your very first step to mental health healing or if you're well-acquainted with therapy and need a supportive booster."

—**Kaitlin Harkess**, clinical psychologist, yoga instructor, and host of the *Wisdom for Wellbeing* podcast

"Liz Kelly's *This Book Is Cheaper Than Therapy* is an engaging and accessible new book helping bridge the gap between peoples' mental health needs and the prospect of engaging direct (often hard-to-find and/or expensive) psychotherapy services. With wit and wisdom, Liz not only guides people toward a better understanding of mental health services but also gives them a sampling of techniques readers can find beneficial before ever stepping in a therapist's office."

—**Mitch Abblett, PhD**, private practice psychologist and author of Nautilus Gold-winning *Prizeworthy*, as well as *The Five Hurdles to Happiness*

"Save your copay and go buy this book! Liz's advice is so smart, sassy, and substantial, you'll almost be glad you didn't find that therapist anyway. She may run me out of a job, but I couldn't be happier. Liz is going to change your life and have you laughing all the way to your best self."

—**Michael Alcée, P**HD, author of *Therapeutic Improvisation: How to Stop Winging It and Own It as a Therapist*

"Liz Kelly's page-turning book reads like an illuminating and nourishing conversation with a supportive friend—who also happens to have a sparkling sense of humor. This text may be cheaper than therapy, but it's chock-full of invaluable insights. With great ease, Kelly links ideas from various schools of psychotherapy to accessible practices you can apply to your everyday life. Whether or not you're able to pursue formal therapy, Liz Kelly's words, both highly informed and entertaining, will empower you to embark on a journey of effective, holistic self-care."

—**Mark O'Connell, LCSW-R**, author of *The Performing Art of Therapy: Acting Insights and Techniques for Clinicians*

"Liz Kelly has packed a substantial collection of powerful mental health tools and strategies into a readable and relatable manual. Readers will feel like they are interacting with a good friend who also happens to be an excellent therapist. Applying these tools will undoubtedly improve mental health and quality of life."

—**Britt H. Rathbone, LCSW-C**, co-author of *What Works With Teens, Parenting a Teen Who Has Intense Emotions*, and other publications

"Medical and therapeutic professionals are waking up to an idea actors have long understood and business professionals have recently discovered: improvisation, specifically applied improvisation, benefits both teams and individuals, helping them 'read the room' and 'be present' for enhanced communication and interpersonal dynamics. In *This Book Is Cheaper Than Therapy*, Liz Kelly takes that a step further: she shows you, using the tools of improvisation, how to be more present for yourself and how to 'read the room' when it comes to your own thoughts and feelings. (Hint: you just might be making them up!) You'll discover tools and skills to better understand yourself, those around you, and how be intentional about your mental and emotional health and well-being."

—**Shawn Westfall**, improv comedy actor and instructor and founder of Westfall Partners

"As the need and demand for therapy grows, Liz Kelly's new book can be a godsend to those who need help right now! Great personal advice laced with humor and authenticity from a down-to-earth therapist. She makes the complexities of therapy easy to understand and apply, with a 'DIY' approach to changing one's life for the better. From extreme self-care to managing emotions and finding the right kind of support, Kelly freely shares a therapeutic mindset to help readers improve their outlook and their lives."

—**Lynn Grodzki**, author of *Therapy with a Coaching Edge*

"Liz Kelly's *This Book Is Cheaper Than Therapy* is a lifeline in the midst of our national mental health crisis. I know Liz as a highly effective therapist. She is also an entertaining writer who delivers therapeutic insights, hope, and validation all woven together with her experience, wisdom, and quick wit. Writing with bravery and compassion, Liz opens doors and minds to the importance of mental wellness using her flair for humor. I'm buying my three twenty-something sons a copy as soon as it is available!"

—**Susan Vitale Greynolds**, LPC, EdD, grief and trauma therapist

"What a gift! Liz has taken the time to write down a perfect 101 course for everyone wanting to feel more sane and grounded in an insane and ungrounded time. This book is full of easy, doable, and extremely powerful ideas and behavioral suggestions that can be absolutely life-changing when adopted. I love that each one is laid out so tangibly, generously, and with Liz's spark of authenticity and vulnerability. I would highly recommend reading this book in addition to or before starting therapy."

—**Paula D. Atkinson**, LICSW, LCSW, E-RYT 500

THIS BOOK IS CHEAPER THAN THERAPY

A No-Nonsense Guide to Improving Your Mental Health

LIZ KELLY, LICSW

Published by
Bridge City Books, an imprint of PESI Publishing, Inc.
3839 White Ave
Eau Claire, WI 54703

Cover and interior design by Emily Dyer
Editing by Jenessa Jackson, PhD

ISBN: 9781962305006 (print)
ISBN: 9781962305013 (ePUB)
ISBN: 9781962305020 (ePDF)

Bridge City Books
An Imprint of PESI Publishing

For Judson Richardson, Carol Bartlett,
Stephanie Handel, and Amy Cirbus

How lucky am I to have found you as mentors.
Thank you for believing in me.
My life is better because you are in it.

AUTHOR'S NOTE

My Social Location

Before going further into this book, I would like to share my social location to give a fuller picture of who I am and what informs my experience, both personally and professionally. I find it important to share this information with you so you can better understand the lens through which I navigate the world. I am a White, cisgender, heterosexual female from the Xennial generation (also known as those of us who grew up playing *Oregon Trail*). I use the pronouns *she/her/hers*. I am married and have two young children. I am originally from small-town Illinois and have spent the last 22 years in the Washington, DC, metro area. I have a master's degree in clinical social work and am currently self-employed as a therapist and writer.

Confidentiality and a Word of Caution

The relationship between a therapist and their client is a special connection. The information my clients disclose during their sessions is confidential and protected by a strict code of ethics and the law. Therefore, the client stories in this book are fictional accounts based on my clinical work as a mental health professional and my personal experiences being human. Any similarities or resemblances to people living or dead are purely coincidental.

The information in this book is for informational purposes only. It is not intended to diagnose, treat, or cure any mental health condition. Despite the cheeky title, this book is not a substitute for medical or mental health treatment. Please discuss any mental health concerns with your doctor or licensed mental health professional. If you are experiencing a mental health crisis and are worried about your safety, don't hesitate to go to the nearest emergency room or dial 988 to reach the National Suicide and Crisis Lifeline.

Finally, you should make a different book selection if you are sensitive to swear words. I believe a few f-bombs are necessary to manage the messiness of life.

CONTENTS

INTRODUCTION

 If you can't fly then run, if you can't run then walk,
if you can't walk then crawl, but whatever you do
you have to keep moving forward.

—Martin Luther King Jr.

You've finally decided to get therapy and improve your mental health. Right on! But then you discover how much it costs to talk with a therapist per hour: about the same as half a plane ticket to Chicago or a pair of really nice shoes from Nordstrom. You thought that maybe insurance would cover mental health treatment, only to find out that your plan doesn't offer that benefit.

Or perhaps you made room in your budget for therapy. You checked out listings on Psychology Today, asked around for some referrals, and started calling therapists to see if they had openings. But everyone has a three-month waiting list. Just what you need when you are feeling down, anxious, and burned out, am I right?

I get it. Finding a good therapist is hard. Finding a good therapist you click with is even more complicated. As a therapist practicing in the Washington, DC, area, I am personally unable to accommodate the number of client referrals that I get every month. It is extremely disheartening when I lack the professional capacity to treat someone reaching out for support. *This Book Is Cheaper Than Therapy* is my way of supporting the individuals I am unable to take on as clients. While this book is not a substitute for treatment by a licensed mental health professional, it *can* equip you with the same strategies and tools I share with clients in my psychotherapy practice.

You deserve to feel better. Feeling better is possible. I know this to be true after witnessing my clients' incredible growth. I am in awe of the courage they bring to the therapy room every day. I also know that change is possible from my own personal experiences. I came to Washington, DC, from the cornfields of southern Illinois after college to do something big. I had visions of working in politics or impacting international policy, but I didn't even know how to work a copier or make decent coffee. I was struggling with undiagnosed depression and unresolved grief. I couldn't have a challenging conversation or speak up for myself without my voice wavering and my eyes tearing up. I relied on bottles of Trader Joe's "Two-Buck Chuck" cabernet sauvignon and jumbo slices of sausage pizza to cope.

This is the book I wish I had then. This book is for my younger self—the person who didn't know that things could get a lot better with therapy, education, self-compassion, a few good friends, and a prescription for Wellbutrin.

What *Is* Therapy Anyway?

Despite what some people think, therapy isn't some form of mystical sorcery. Therapists don't have a magic wand or anything like that—usually just lots of coffee. Rather, therapy is a tool that lets you see what is going well and not so well in your life and that helps you identify your strengths and vulnerabilities. It's a safe space for you to be human. It allows you to shed light on your insecurities, negative thoughts, and unhealthy patterns of behavior without judgment or criticism. From there, you can take steps to make positive changes.

Therapy also provides you with some accountability as you take those initial first steps toward positive change. Change is hard, and it's not always linear. Our brains love to gravitate toward what feels comfortable and familiar, even if what is comfortable and familiar is not the best for us. (This is why I want to eat chocolate pecan caramels instead of going for a walk.) Therapy provides a place to figure out these obstacles to positive change. As my glamorous middle-school choir teacher, Mrs. Swickard, was known to say, "Cope and adjust." That's what therapy does: It helps you cope and adjust as you figure out how to best navigate the challenges that life throws your way.

In a typical session, a therapist will ask you questions, help you identify personal goals, offer nonjudgmental support, reflect on the patterns and themes they glean from your conversations, and provide feedback. Therapy is a place that allows you to share the details of your life without being judged as weird, crazy, out of control, or annoying. It is 100 percent for you. Your session is all about *your* needs and *your* goals. It's one hour per week to focus entirely on your mental well-being.

And the reality is that we could all use some therapy after dealing with the social, political, and economic upheaval of these past few years. And that's on top of things like managing a worldwide pandemic, wearing pants, dating, keeping up with the laundry, and trying to get through your 27th Zoom meeting of the day. It's a lot. Everyone needs to be supported and validated. And that includes therapists too—just like you, they also struggle with their own challenges. If you need proof that therapists don't always have it together, I cut myself peeling a hard-boiled egg earlier today. The current state of my living room can only be described as "there appears to have been a struggle." And my four-year-old has refused to brush her hair for the past eight days and is slowly starting to resemble a feral child. Therapists aren't perfect, but we do study resilience and have some strategies on how to deal with this thing called life.

How This Book Can Help

Maybe I have been watching too many true-crime dramas lately, but I like to think of myself as a bit of a detective when I start working with a client. In my first session with them, I will consider the many factors that can impact a person's mental well-being, including their level of physical activity, relationships, use of technology, work-life balance, previous life experiences, physical health, and overall lifestyle. The wheels turn in my head as I attempt to identify what might be increasing this person's anxiety and stress levels or dragging down their mood and energy.

The good news is you don't have to see a therapist to perform this same sort of assessment on yourself. You can do this by engaging in self-reflection, attending to the mind-body connection, learning to manage your emotions, establishing boundaries, and creating meaning in your life through the tools in this book. In fact, here's a little-known fact about therapy: The real work happens outside the session. Change happens when you gain insight into yourself and practice new ways of being in the world.

Although I can't take away your problems or pain, I can offer suggestions to help you escape the rabbit hole of suffering more quickly. However, please keep in mind that not every suggestion will work for everyone. One person might benefit from practicing meditation, while another might benefit from lifting heavy weights while listening to loud music at the gym. Since you are unique, your specific prescription for optimum mental health will also be unique. Therefore, as you read this book, I encourage you to choose a few different strategies, give them an honest try, and see what works for you. If you try a technique and it's not for you, that's okay! Feel free to disregard it and try something else. This is your life. Stay true to what works for you—not what works for your mother, your sister, your friend, your boss, that social media influencer you follow, or that celebrity you read about in *People* magazine.

I also know that change can seem challenging when you feel stuck, burned out, or emotionally drained. You are not alone in feeling that way. Know that small actions over time lead to meaningful change. You do not need to make sweeping changes to your life overnight. Celebrate every small decision you make that leads to positive change. Your worth is not in any way connected to your productivity or accomplishments.

You are enough right now. I also don't believe that finding yourself is a "one-and-done" process. We all get off track sometimes. Your priorities today might look different in the future, and that's okay. You can always find yourself again and learn something in the process. I hope this book will help you do just that.

CHAPTER 1

SELF-CARE IS SURVIVAL

 My mission in life is not merely to survive, but to thrive; and to do so with some passion, some compassion, some humor, and some style.

—Maya Angelou

Self-Care Is a Radical Act of Survival

I could be the best therapist in the world when it comes to having the latest therapeutic interventions; still, those interventions won't do a darn thing if you are sleep deprived, subsisting on Oreos and cheeseburgers, drinking four beers a day, or spending 12 hours a day on your phone. Learning to examine your thoughts and core beliefs is important, but you can't neglect the basics of self-care.

I was in graduate school for social work the first time I heard the term *self-care*. My professors were trying to make sure that we baby therapists didn't become vicariously traumatized by the challenging stories of our clients and the limitations of the agencies where we interned. My professors hoped to instill in us the healthy habits critical to remaining engaged and present with clients.

But I got self-care completely wrong back then. I thought it meant doing things that felt good or treating myself. I would get $30 pedicures that I couldn't afford, eat Five Guys cheeseburgers and fries, and drink a couple of glasses of wine at night. I thought that was going to make me feel less stressed. Turns out it made me feel hungover and bloated, with pretty feet and a higher credit card balance.

It took me some time to figure out what authentic self-care is. I eventually realized that self-care is about mindfully taking the time to do things that help you survive on a day-to-day basis, which is not always sexy or fun. It's about taking actions that improve your health for the long haul and that recharge you mentally, physically, and emotionally, whether that's setting boundaries with a family member who always comes over unannounced, turning off your email notifications when you clock out of work, or going to bed early instead of staying up late in an attempt to make up for lost leisure time (a phenomenon known as revenge bedtime procrastination). True self-care facilitates long-term health and wellness, not just what feels good in the moment. You can think of your energy, patience, and overall mental wellness as money in your bank account: Some activities deplete your account, while self-care activities replenish your account.

In this chapter, I'll dispel some common misconceptions about self-care, describe the many different forms of self-care that exist, and teach you how to successfully implement self-care in practice.

Common Myths of Self-Care

The term *self-care* has been a buzzword lately on social media and in pop culture. Self-care is everywhere! Google Search Trends showed a 250 percent increase in self-care–related searches between 2019 and 2020,[1] and the global wellness market is now worth an estimated $1.5 trillion.[2] As a result, there are now entire magazines and television shows devoted to the concept of self-care. Retailers know that people are all looking for ways to feel better and care for themselves. Gwyneth Paltrow and her company, Goop, even had an entire Netflix series covering the latest wellness trends. But despite our society's current preoccupation with self-care, myths continue to swirl about the concept.

Myth #1: Self-Care Is Selfish

Taking care of ourselves can feel selfish. Often, we are so focused on giving to others—being a good parent, employee, spouse, family member, friend, or community member—that we forget to make ourselves a priority. Women, in particular, are culturally conditioned to care for others at their own expense. As Emily and Amelia Nagoski eloquently explain in their book, *Burnout: The Secret to Unlocking the Stress Cycle*, women are expected to be pretty, calm, generous, and attentive to the needs of others at all times. That responsibility can feel overwhelming.

The reality is that self-care is necessary so you can thrive and have the energy to be an engaged and active member of society. You are not depriving someone else by prioritizing your own needs. You can't take care of others without taking care of yourself first. It's like flying on an airplane: In the event that there is a change in cabin pressure, the flight attendant will tell you to put on your oxygen mask first before assisting others. Self-care is your metaphorical oxygen mask for life.

Myth #2: Self-Care Is Expensive, Time-Consuming, and Only for Women

Scrolling through social media and watching reality television would make you believe that self-care requires spending big bucks on a personal trainer and green smoothies. In Western culture, television shows like *The Real Housewives* promote the image of self-care as something only attainable by wealthy White women. This has made self-care synonymous with expensive spa treatments at exclusive resorts or fancy trips to wineries with groups of girlfriends. And while those things are nice (I confess to regularly paying way too much for ginger kombucha at the Fresh Market), they are certainly not a prerequisite for good mental and physical health.

If you are looking to take better care of yourself, you don't need to buy expensive aromatherapy kits, detox bath soaps, eye masks to help you sleep, fancy journals, or CBD oil. You don't need any of those things for self-care, but if you want to buy yourself some healing crystals, knock yourself out. (Full disclosure, I am that person who buys the healing crystals. I have all the crystals. I can't resist a pretty rock that claims to help me increase my intuition and find inner peace.)

In contrast, authentic self-care involves taking small, sustainable actions that rejuvenate your body and mind regardless of your age, gender, race, sexual identity, or socioeconomic status. Self-care can look like making time for showers and haircuts, creating a budget, or getting enough sleep. Self-care could involve going on a walk around the block at lunch or sending a "thinking of you" text to a friend.

If you are overwhelmed and busy with life, it might feel like engaging in any of these forms of self-care is impossible. It can be tough to take care of yourself when the demands of life are intense. But it is possible to incorporate small actions to help yourself feel better. Even taking mindful, deep breaths while waiting in line at Walgreens or taking five minutes to get a glass of water can be considered self-care.

Myth #3: Self-Care Is Unnecessary

Hustle culture has given everyone the idea that we should constantly be working at the expense of our own needs if we really want to be successful. If you spend just a few minutes scrolling through Instagram, you'll likely encounter various hustle-culture memes that broadcast platitudes like "Rise and grind," "Find your passion," and "Live your dream." Am I the only one getting heartburn here? That's a lot of pressure. I don't know about you, but I don't want to be grinding every day. Sometimes I want to rise and lounge.

I remember idealizing the phrase "Work hard, play hard" when I first entered the professional world. I internalized the message that needing rest and downtime meant I was weak. That I constantly needed to do more. That I should deny my own basic needs and push through. However, the reality is that doing more and neglecting your own needs isn't a recipe for success—it's a recipe for burnout. When you are always focused on the grind, you forget to enjoy where you are right now. You fail to take care of yourself for the long haul. In addition, when you are always focused on the next big thing, it's hard to show up and be present for the people in your life.

Self-care is not something you have to earn by being productive and checking off all the items on your to-do list. You are not "weak" if you practice self-care. In actuality, practicing self-care is a sign of strength. It shows you value yourself.

Myth #4: Self-Care Is Anything That Feels Good

Our brains will always gravitate toward the quick hit of pleasure that comes from checking social media, clicking that "buy now" button, or grabbing a craft beer from the fridge after a long day. And there is nothing wrong with enjoying a delicious chocolate cupcake or watching a few videos on TikTok every so often. Treats are certainly something that can be incorporated into a balanced life.

The problem comes when you over-rely on activities that make you feel good now but worse later. Quick fixes can't become your default methods of coping. There is a distinct difference between numbing out versus restoring yourself. It all comes down to your motivation for doing an activity. Are you watching television because you enjoy the show and find it engaging? Or are you so overwhelmed from the day that you want to binge-watch a series and not feel anything? Are you giving full attention to that delicious slice of carrot cake and enjoying every bite? Or are you frantically shoveling down French fries to get some comfort from a stressful day? Many things that feel good in the moment do not lead to long-term health or satisfaction.

Likewise, many things that *don't* necessarily feel good or pleasurable in the moment *are* forms of self-care. This can include meal prepping veggies for the week, waking up early to work out, and scheduling that annual physical with your doctor.

Myth #5: Self-Care Is the Same as Self-Improvement

Our culture loves a good makeover story. Bookshelves and magazines are full of suggestions on how to be different, look different, and improve yourself. I, too, am a total sucker for any show that culminates in a jaw-dropping before-and-after closet renovation. But self-care is not the same as self-improvement. In contrast to the goal of self-improvement, which is to become a better version of yourself, the concept of self-care accepts and honors the person you are right now. Although self-care may lead to positive change over time, it's not the goal. You are worthy of attention and care *right now*, just as you are.

For example, I used to exercise because I was trying to live up to unrealistic beauty standards that told me I had to look a certain way and be a smaller size (thanks to the lack of body diversity in all those shiny airbrushed magazine ads in the '90s and 2000s). I used to think that physical activity didn't count if I wasn't burning a ton of calories, but all movement is beneficial. (Currently shaking my head at my younger self, who didn't see the benefit in all types of movement. Sigh.) Now I engage in physical activity because it's how I manage stress, boost my mood, and gain the strength to do the things I enjoy. I move for the fun of it and will never turn down an impromptu dance party.

Types of Self-Care

There are several different types of self-care, including physical, mental, emotional, spiritual, recreational, financial, and professional. In this section, I'll help you get a better understanding of what each category involves, since people often do well with addressing self-care needs in some parts of their lives but not so well in others. For example, you might be crushing your career goals and successfully training for that 10k you've always wanted to run, but you aren't making time to check in with your best bud from college or keeping adequate track of your finances. Going over these different types of self-care can help you identify the parts of your life that could use more attention.

Physical Self-Care

Physical self-care is anything that supports your physical health and wellness. This can include attending regular medical appointments and visiting the dentist twice a year. Activities like wearing your seatbelt, practicing safe sex, and drinking water fall into this category as well. Getting adequate nutrition, physical activity, and sleep are also essential for regulating your emotions and stabilizing your mood. Since these three areas in particular are your first line of defense when it comes to feeling good, they warrant special attention.

Nutrition

Your gut is home to trillions of microorganisms that help with everything from digesting your food to supporting your immune system. Research in the past decade has shown that these microbiomes can influence how you feel through what is known as the gut-brain axis, which is a bidirectional communication system between your gastrointestinal tract and your brain. In fact, the gut is sometimes referred to as the "second brain" because of its influence on mental health.

So what does this mean for you? It means that improving the health of your gastrointestinal system can improve your mood. And you can do this by making changes to your diet that reduce inflammation in the gastrointestinal system—for example, eating fermented foods, consuming more fiber, embracing the Mediterranean diet, and supplementing with probiotics and prebiotics. Although research on the gut-brain axis is still developing, making these dietary changes can potentially reduce anxiety and depression symptoms.

Preventing blood sugar spikes and dips can also help you better manage your mental well-being. You can keep your blood sugar more stable by increasing the amount of protein and fiber in your diet and decreasing your intake of simple carbs and sweets. If mornings are tough for you, do you need to change your breakfast to something more sustaining? Instead of reaching for your morning blueberry muffin or cereal, what about eating something packed with more protein, like an omelet or Greek yogurt? Or perhaps you need to focus on eating more regularly throughout the day.

Reflecting on your eating habits can give important insight into your mental well-being. But always consult your primary care doctor or a registered dietician before making significant changes to your diet. Good mental and physical health takes a village.

Physical Activity

Exercise is often viewed as something you need to do to look a certain way or lose weight. Screw that! You don't need to exercise to shrink your body or try to live up to some impossible standard. Exercise should not be a punishment for your body because you ate a "bad" food. (The only foods that are bad for you are moldy, expired, or give you gas.)

Instead, it's time to reframe the concept of physical activity. As author and health educator Emily Nagoski says, "Physical activity is the single most efficient strategy for completing the stress response cycle."[3] All that tension that builds up in your body during the day? Exercise is how you can release it. If you want to play music and dance around your apartment, that's exercise. Doing yard work, cleaning your house, stretching, and walking all count as physical activity. You can even stand up next to your desk after a stressful phone call and shake your arms, legs, and body—literally shake out the tension. If you want to do more physical activity, rock on!

The options are endless. Prioritize moving your body in a way that feels good to you. Start with whatever movement feels manageable and go from there. I want you to exercise because you love yourself and deserve those happy endorphins.

Sleep and Rest

I once traveled to Greece with my friend Christina. We were on the island of Mykonos, which is known as the party island. After a certain point, I told Christina that I planned to call it a night and return to our bed and breakfast, to which she emphatically replied, "You can sleep when you're dead!" So I ignored my exhaustion, and we went off to a club called Cavo Paradiso on the side of a cliff. On our way home at 7:00 a.m., we passed a few elderly Orthodox Greek women on their way to church, and I am pretty sure a few of them made the sign of the cross as we passed by.

Nowadays, my idea of partying is grabbing takeout from my favorite Thai place, getting lost in a good book, firing up my aromatherapy diffuser, and getting a solid eight hours of sleep. In fact, I wish sleep were considered a hobby because I am great at it. But most of us don't get enough. Although the average adult typically needs between seven and nine hours of sleep each night, many people find themselves staying up late to watch just one more episode of their favorite Netflix show rather than listening to their bodies' cues that they are tired and need to go to bed. Other people work nights and have a sleep schedule that's constantly changing. And some people wake up at night and stare at the ceiling with 1,000 thoughts running through their minds. These things make it tough to get quality rest.

To improve sleep quality, you'll want to keep technology out of the bedroom and avoid screens right before bed. This will reduce the powerful temptation to watch "just one more" episode, shop online, answer text messages, or scroll through social media. I have totally been there. A couple of years ago, I fell into the habit of staying up too late to watch YouTube videos of Mount Everest explorers. I have no idea why, other than I wanted to see whose nose and toes would get frostbitten first. I don't like the cold and I am 100 percent certain that I will never climb Mount Everest. The YouTube rabbit hole is easy to fall into. Apps and social media are engineered to suck you in and keep you engaged.

The single most effective hack I have found for improving sleep is to charge your phone outside your bedroom and use an old-school alarm clock to wake up. I usually charge my phone in the bathroom or kitchen. You might feel strange the first night, like you are naked or missing a limb, but sit with the discomfort of not having your phone in the bedroom and see what you notice after a few nights. Chances are you will be sleeping more soundly.

You can also try doing a "brain dump" before going to bed. Grab a sheet of paper, give yourself a minute or two, and freewrite everything in your head. Write down all your to-dos, concerns, and nagging thoughts. Pay no attention to spelling or punctuation and get it all out. Once that's done, you can allow the paper to hold all your worries until morning. (Disclaimer: Avoid this activity if it stirs up anxious feelings or leads to thought spirals.)

In addition to getting quality sleep, make sure to prioritize resting your body *and* mind. The idea of rest can be challenging in a culture that often ties people's worthiness to their levels of productivity. In fact, it's common for people to think that they have to "earn" their rest. You might tell yourself that you can go to bed after you get one last task done or finish cleaning up the kitchen, but rest is not something that has to be earned. You aren't lazy if you need a break! This is how you recharge your brain and body.

You can rest by taking a break from your normal routine. Enjoy a moment of solitude. Spend time in nature. Disconnect from your electronic devices. Turn down social invitations that don't serve you.

Take a reprieve from your responsibilities. Give yourself permission to not be helpful or productive.

Mental Self-Care

Mental self-care is about engaging in activities that spark your intellectual and creative side. This can include anything that you find stimulating, such as doing a puzzle, pursuing a new hobby, playing chess, listening to a podcast, learning a new skill, journaling, reading a book, painting, or taking that online class you've always wanted to try. Mental self-care can help clear your head and nurture your mind when you feel like you're stuck in a rut. It's hard to get out of bed in the morning when you have nothing to look forward to and feel stagnant. Practicing mental self-care can help you avoid getting into this funk.

Emotional Self-Care

Many of us only recognize four basic emotions—mad, sad, happy, and scared—but there is an entire spectrum of emotions. Emotional self-care involves learning to name and express what you are feeling. By naming what you feel, you can lessen that emotion's power over you. You can then act in ways to navigate that emotion more effectively. If naming your emotions is difficult, there are tons of emotion charts online, or you can buy a copy from Etsy or Amazon. A client of mine even found a colorful throw pillow with different emotions printed on it. Try asking yourself throughout the day, *What am I feeling right now?* You might feel a combination of emotions (e.g., bored, tired, excited, content), which is normal.

If you typically find it difficult to control your emotions or are easily triggered, make it a point to integrate this type of self-care into your routine. Many people find that journaling, reciting positive affirmations, meditating, reading motivational books, and going to therapy are helpful ways to focus on emotional self-care. You can also become more in tune with your emotions by developing a gratitude practice in which you identify what you appreciate about yourself, others, and your life. In chapter 4, you'll learn emotional regulation strategies such as this and more.

Spiritual Self-Care

Spiritual self-care is any activity that deepens your connection with something greater than yourself. This doesn't have to involve meditating on a mountaintop for hours unless you are really into that. It also doesn't have to involve religion, though it can. Everyone expresses their spirituality in different ways. One person may find that volunteering, meditating, and spending time in nature are meaningful. Another person might gravitate toward art, a faith community, a church family, prayer, dance, or singing. You do you. All that matters is that you feel a sense of meaning and connection to something bigger than yourself.

Recreational Self-Care

Recreational self-care is all about making time for activities and hobbies that bring you pleasure and enjoyment. It's all about having fun! What are your likes and dislikes? Whom do you like to spend time with? So often, we participate in activities because we *think* we should enjoy them (even though, deep down, we really don't). For example, I played on my company's softball team in my early 20s because that's what everyone did. After a couple of years, I finally had the guts to admit that I hate softball and can't catch a ball to save my life. I am good at bringing snacks, so from then on, I handed out orange slices and drinks at the cooler. I still got to wear the company T-shirt and have a sense of belonging from being on the team, but I no longer had the stress of (literally) dropping the ball. To practice recreational self-care, think about what activities bring you joy, and aim to incorporate more of *that* in your life.

Financial Self-Care

Financial self-care is about developing healthy spending and saving habits that set you up for success. This can look like creating a budget, advocating for the salary you deserve, and starting an emergency fund for those unexpected expenses that inevitably pop up in life. It can also involve planning for retirement, paying bills on time, and not spending money you don't have. Financial self-care also might look like politely turning down an invitation to a friend's wedding or extravagant birthday bash halfway across the country because you'd have to finance the whole trip on a credit card. Going out to that hot French restaurant with friends is only fun if you aren't worried about how you will pay off your steak frites later.

Professional Self-Care

Professional self-care entails taking actions that help you feel supported and balanced in your job and career. This might involve working with a mentor at work or attending a professional development workshop to learn new skills. It might look like eating lunch away from your desk, unplugging from your email after hours, and taking PTO when you need it. Professional self-care is also about recognizing when your current work environment isn't a good fit and interviewing for jobs at organizations that better suit your values and personality.

Figuring Out Your Self-Care Needs

My good friend and fellow therapist Dr. Susan Greynolds and I were talking recently about how we dislike the term *self-care* because it gets misconstrued. The term has been co-opted by capitalism to sell us shit we don't need. To counter that, she said she frequently asks clients, "What does your soul need?" That question can help you determine what kind of self-care would benefit you at that current moment. Your soul might need something simple, like taking a 10-minute nap, or something more complicated, like getting out of a toxic relationship. But you won't know unless you check in with yourself regularly and ask.

Another way to figure out your self-care needs is to ask yourself what would make your life 5 or 10 percent less stressful right now. Take the pressure off yourself in thinking you have to fix or overhaul everything. Instead, get into the habit of identifying what small actions might make things just a tiny bit better. You might feel less stressed if you unload the dishwasher before going to bed at night. Or perhaps you might feel more refreshed if you go for a short walk during your lunch break before diving back into a complex work project. Start small.

Effective Self-Care in Practice

To start making the necessary changes to implement more self-care in your daily life, you have to start by identifying what changes are truly in your control. Many people think they can control everything in life if they do everything "right" and plan for every possible scenario. I hate to burst your bubble here, but there will always be things out of your control. You can't control the weather, traffic on I-95, what other people think, what your friends do, bills, taxes, or death. That really sucks, I know.

I watched the delightful show *Somebody Somewhere* on HBO the other day. My favorite character, Fred Rococo, said, "Control the controllables." He is on to something. You have power over whom you spend time with, what you look at online, what habits you cultivate, what tasks you include in your daily routine, where you spend your money, whether you decide to keep an umbrella in your car, and more. Even when life feels out of control, you have some agency to take positive action.

For example, my client Clara recently had to have a biopsy following an inconclusive mammogram result. She was naturally shaken and didn't know how she would handle the few days until the results came back. Her thoughts started to spiral as she reflected on what could happen in the future. Clara took some deep breaths and asked herself what was in her control. No, she couldn't control the outcome of the biopsy. But she could focus on taking care of herself by getting enough sleep, fueling herself with healthy meals, clearing her head on walks outside, and keeping busy by doing a closet cleanout. These small steps helped her find some stability until she received the good news that she was cancer-free.

To start making *controllable* changes in your life, reflect on what you would like your ideal day to look like. What would you do in the morning? How would your day flow? What activities would occupy your evening? See if you can make one small part of your ideal day a reality. But don't try to overhaul your entire routine at once. Set yourself up for success by making one small change and then another. For example, if you envisioned an ideal morning to include waking up with enough time to read the news and drink coffee, try setting your alarm 15 minutes earlier this week. Maybe even set up your coffee maker the night before. Then see how it feels to have that daily ritual.

Many clients also find it helpful to have "check-in" and "check-out" rituals before and after work. A check-in ritual might involve the following:

- Drinking coffee and water
- Reviewing your schedule for the day
- Rewriting your to-do list
- Figuring out your top three priorities for the day

A check-out ritual might involve:

- Identifying your high and low points of the day
- Straightening your desk before leaving work

- Reflecting on what you accomplished

- Listening to your favorite music after work

The point of these rituals is to help you better transition between your personal and professional life, which is especially important during a time when the boundaries between work and home have become increasingly blurred. These rituals provide a sense of safety and security. We like knowing what comes next. Many of us feel lost and uncertain without this external structure and routine.

Self-Care Hacks When You Feel Anxious or Down

I am no stranger to putting things off. I even have a set of pencils that say "Just fucking do it already." When you feel anxious or depressed, it can be tough to get going or think clearly. (I'll explain why this is the case in the following chapters.) This can make it challenging to engage in self-care activities that could potentially make you feel better. Fortunately, a few hacks can help you take positive action when stress feels overwhelming or symptoms of anxiety or depression surface.

Figure Out Your Top Three Tasks

To-do lists are great, but it can be easy to fall into the trap of putting too many things on your list. Ask yourself, *What would make today feel successful or meaningful? What do I need to do to have a good day today?* Your answers to these questions reflect your top priorities. Focus on two or three of these priorities and go from there.

For example, my client Marcela was a successful graphic designer, but she often felt like she wasn't doing enough and vented about being overloaded with tasks. She would look at her to-do list at the end of each day and feel like a failure because she didn't get through everything.

She then began taking a few minutes each morning to reflect on what would need to happen to have a good day. For example, a typical day might include spending time with her kids, completing the first draft of a promotional brochure for a nonprofit client, and sending out invoices. When Marcela began to focus on these priorities, she began to see progress and recognize what she had accomplished instead of what wasn't getting done.

Break It Down

Once you have identified your top two or three priorities, break those tasks down into even smaller steps. I am talking about tiny, micro, baby steps. Often the most challenging part of accomplishing a task is getting started. If you can make getting started easier, that's half the battle. For example, I deal with lots of note-taking and documentation as a therapist. This is not my favorite part of my job, but it's a necessary evil. To actually get my paperwork done, I have been known to break this task down by writing the following on a sheet of paper:

Step 1: Make coffee.

Step 2: Drink the coffee.

Step 3: Open the computer.

Step 4: Open the client database.

Step 5: Write notes.

I get a sense of satisfaction that comes from checking things off. Make the coffee, check! Drink the coffee and done! I'm crushing it.

Use a Planner

Some of you probably came out of the womb with a planner or digital app for organizing. But if you aren't one of those natural-born organizers, consider writing down your to-do list each day. Spend time updating your schedule and calendar. Rather than trying to keep it all in your head and getting stressed when you forget a task, put all that info in one place. Find a system that works for you, whether that's posting a bunch of sticky notes on your fridge, using a fancy three-ring binder, or religiously updating your electronic calendar.

Try Single Tasking and the Timer Trick

I'm not too fond of multitasking and don't believe in it. Sorry, not sorry. Multitasking is *not* about doing two things at the same time. It's about rapidly switching from one activity to another. And every time you switch to a different activity, you have to refocus. This takes up precious time and energy.

The alternative to multitasking is single tasking: You only do one thing at a time. A way to embrace single tasking is to use a timer. Set a timer for five or ten minutes and give your entire focus to that task. Don't check email or text messages during this time or get up to grab a snack or glass of water. Work for five or ten minutes straight, without distraction, and see how it feels. You may surprise yourself with how much you accomplish.

For example, a client of mine, Terence, lived by himself in a typical Washington, DC, efficiency apartment with no dishwasher. His kitchen would often get cluttered with dirty dishes, leading him to feel totally overwhelmed and setting off a spiral of negative thoughts and feelings. "My kitchen is a mess. I am a mess. I am so unproductive. I can't get anything done. No one would ever want to come over to my apartment." In turn, he would feel even worse, which led to him ordering takeout and distracting himself with his phone. And the kitchen would stay cluttered.

Then Terence tried the timer trick. Even though he didn't feel like cleaning his kitchen, he told himself that it was just five minutes of his day and that he could do anything for five minutes. Terence was stunned that he could wash all the dishes in his sink in this time frame, so he set the timer again. This time he was able to dry all the dishes. Before he knew it, his kitchen was clean, and he experienced a sense of accomplishment that he hadn't felt in a long time. He felt energized and went out to buy some groceries and try a new pasta recipe.

Setting the timer for just five minutes triggered a chain of positive reactions for Terence. You, too, can experience this positive change for yourself. Begin single tasking by starting small. Start with five minutes and work your way up. You are training your attention span, similar to how you would train your muscles by lifting weights at the gym.

Use Body Doubling (a.k.a. Bring a Friend)

Body doubling involves completing a task in the company of another person. Many people find it easier to focus when there is someone else there. The presence of another person can make the work more entertaining, help you stay on task, and give you a source of positive feedback. Body doubling might look like doing household chores with your roommate, studying with a classmate, or having a friend hang out with you while you organize your closet. One caveat, though: Choose your company wisely! I have a few friends whom I love dearly but who will be a source of distraction to me. I know that we will end up chatting and eating chips and salsa rather than doing anything of substance.

Get Smart with Your Cold, Hard Cash

Managing finances is an essential component of self-care and maintaining your mental health. You may (or may not) be surprised that the subject of money comes up often in therapy sessions as a common source of stress. Money is emotional and frequently tied to our value systems, and how we spend and save is often related to our experiences with money as children and young adults. For example, several of my clients grew up in households where they experienced financial insecurity, which informs how they interact with money today. Many have a fear of spending money, even if they are financially well-off, or they stick their head in the sand about financial matters because thinking about money is uncomfortable. Other clients spend impulsively and excessively when treating themselves because they often had to go without money as kids.

I often talk to my clients about becoming more intentional with their money by identifying financial goals that are in line with their values and that would bring them long-term meaning, security, or happiness. One strategy that many of my clients have found helpful to curb impulse spending is to ask themselves a series of questions before they make a purchase. Some even print out these questions on a card and post it next to their computer or stash it in their wallet. These questions could include:

- Is this something I need?

- Can I wait a day to make this purchase?

- Can I afford this without taking on debt?

- Do I really want to make space in my home for this?

- Will this thing continue to bring me joy or happiness in a week, a month, or a year?

- Will this purchase delay a more meaningful financial goal like going on vacation, starting my own business, creating an emergency fund, or funding my retirement?

Be Your Own Cheerleader

Many people seek external validation as a way to feel happy with life. They desperately want a positive review from their boss, an A+ on that paper, or a bunch of likes on their recent Instagram post. Although external validation feels great, it's not something you can control.

You can, however, control the validation you give yourself. See what it's like to cheer yourself on throughout the day. If you unload the dishwasher, tell yourself, *Great work!* If you led a meeting at work (or even if you simply stayed awake during a meeting at work), say, *Well done!* I usually give myself internal validation in my head (so as not to weird out my spouse and kids), but feel free to say these things out loud if you really feel it.

Mel Robbins, a motivational speaker, discusses the benefits of validating yourself in her book *The High 5 Habit*. She suggests giving your reflection a high five in the mirror as a strategy to cheer yourself on and reduce self-doubt. High-fiving yourself might sound a little strange at first, but it's an easy way to give yourself a boost anytime you pass by a mirror.

Action Items

1. Take some time to reflect on the different areas of your life that could use attention (physical, mental, emotional, spiritual, recreational, financial, and professional). What areas are going well? What areas are you neglecting?

2. Identify three ways to intentionally incorporate self-care into your week.

3. Think about the day ahead. What could you do between now and the end of the day to look back and say, "I had a great day"?

4. What are some things in life that you can control? What would give you a greater sense of stability?

CHAPTER 2

MEET YOUR INNER CRITIC

 You've been criticizing yourself for years and it hasn't worked. Try approving of yourself and see what happens.

—Louise L. Hay

Meet Nelson

Everyone has an inner critic, that little voice in your head that criticizes you, puts you down, and tells you to do more. Your inner critic can be incredibly mean. Often, your inner critic sounds a lot like someone from your past who may have been hard on you, like a parent, bully, teacher, or coach. Your inner critic is also greatly influenced by your culture, your family, your community, your upbringing, and even what you see on social media and advertisements. For example, suppose your mom tended to be a people pleaser who always put others' needs before her own. In that case, you may have developed an inner critic who harps on you for not being selfless enough or who makes you feel like you can't say no to requests.

My inner critic's name is Nelson. I decided to give that critical voice a name a couple of years ago to make it easier for me to talk back and challenge that constant source of negativity. Nelson is simply a personification of the negative thoughts that run through my head. (Nothing against any lovely people out there who are named Nelson. If you want to name your inner critic Liz, I won't take offense.)

Nelson and I are on pretty good terms lately. It took practice, but I do an excellent job of keeping him in his place now. It wasn't always this way, however. When I was in my early 20s, Nelson was a constant presence. (I just didn't have a name for my negative thoughts back then.) My internal dialogue would often sound a lot like this:

When feeling stuck on a project at work:

NELSON: You can't ask for help. Everyone will think you are stupid! And everyone is busy. You should just figure it out yourself.

LIZ: But I really don't know how to do this task, and it's taking a really long time. I might miss my deadline or do it wrong.

NELSON: Big whoop. Deal with it, sister. Asking for help is weak. You should be smart enough to figure this out on your own.

LIZ: Um . . . okay.

(Cut to me turning in a project late and sloppy because Nelson wouldn't let me ask for help.)

While shopping for clothes at the mall:

LIZ: This is a cute dress.

NELSON: Slow your roll, girl. That makes you look fat. Why aren't you working out more anyway? You're lazy.

LIZ: Yeah, I guess maybe I should work out more . . .

NELSON: Why don't you look as good as your friend Louise? She looks awesome.

LIZ: Yeah, but she has a totally different body type than I do. Her ancestors must have been Swedish glamazons or something. My ancestors were sturdy German and Irish farmers built to harvest potatoes.

NELSON: Don't care. If you just tried harder and ate better, you could look like the models in those ads over there.

(Cut to me buying shoes I didn't need and drowning my sorrows in an extra-large sausage breakfast burrito because I felt like crap about myself.)

While hanging out with a guy I liked:

LIZ: I wonder if he likes me. Maybe I should ask him out?

NELSON: No way! He's too good for you.

LIZ: But we seem to get along.

NELSON: Whatever. You aren't hot enough or outgoing enough for him.

LIZ: Yeah, you are probably right. Better play it safe.

(Cut to me being dateless on Friday night.)

As you can see, inner critics can be quite the troublemakers and hold you back. So why do you have this voice in your head anyway? It all goes back to something called the negativity bias, which refers to the brain's tendency to pay more attention to bad things in the environment than the good. For example, you can probably think of a performance review you had in the past where your boss told you a dozen positive things about your work but then mentioned a few teensy areas for improvement. Your brain probably immediately disregarded all the fantastic, glowing feedback and hyperfocused on that one negative point, right? That's the negativity bias at work.

The negativity bias reflects your brain's misguided attempt to protect you. It goes back to the caveman days. Think about it: If you were standing in the tundra gazing at butterflies, rainbows, and sunshine, a saber tooth tiger could jump out and gobble you up. There goes any chance of passing your genes on to future generations! You just became part of the circle of life. To survive, your ancestors had to pay close attention to anything unsettling in their surroundings so they could avoid danger. As a result, your brain is wired from an evolutionary and functional perspective to pay close attention to the negative, even in modern-day society.

Unreasonable Expectations from Society

Your inner critic reflects the internalized expectations placed on you by society. You constantly face subtle messages about who you "should" be and how you "should" act. Taming your inner critic is thus a process of unlearning the many messages you have received from your family and friends, your religion and faith traditions, popular culture, entertainment, and social media. To dismantle unreasonable expectations placed on you by society, you must gain awareness of what those expectations are. It's time to pause and reflect rather than continue to blindly follow a set of arbitrary and often conflicting rules.

To gain insight into your experience, consider the following:

- What are you told that your body is supposed to look like? What are the expectations regarding your appearance?

- Who is expected to make the most money in your household?

- What do people expect of you emotionally? Do you always have to be strong? Or is it okay for you to cry or show emotion?

- Are you allowed to accept help from others or rely on others for support?

- Do you feel pressured to always be nice and accommodating? Or is it acceptable for you to disregard others' feelings and act in your own self-interest?

- How are you expected to handle conflict? Do you feel like you always need to have the last word? Or are you expected to keep the peace at all costs?

- How have you been taught that you "should" feel about sex? Are you expected to express (or suppress) your sexuality?

- Are you expected to lead or follow?

- Do you have permission to be vulnerable and open with your friends? Or are you expected to keep conversations at a surface level?

- Do you feel like you're supposed to follow a spiritual calling to be a parent? Or is being a parent simply one part of your identity?

- Is your worth defined by your relationship or marital status?

- Do you have permission to make mistakes?

- Are you expected to carry the majority of the emotional labor in your home (e.g., remembering important dates, caregiving for children and elders, taking care of household chores, cooking, being the historian or photographer)?

- What does a "good" member of your faith look like?

Once you gain awareness of the societal expectations that you have been pressured to meet, you can recognize the futility of trying to be all things at once. You can reject a standard that doesn't work for you. You can give yourself permission to disregard the rigid rules about what you "should" be. I acknowledge that it's much easier for some groups to safely break societal norms than it is for others because the playing field isn't level. (More on that in a second.) Still, no one benefits when they have to contort themselves to fit external expectations. Belonging is not about fitting in. It is about finding acceptance for who you are.

The Playing Field Isn't Level

Growing up in a small Midwestern town lacking racial, religious, and economic diversity, I naively grew up thinking that our country's playing field is level. I am ashamed that I foolishly believed in the American dream of everyone having equal access to opportunity. The story I bought into is that anyone in the United States can succeed with motivation and talent. I assumed that my accomplishments were a result of only my abilities and merit and not my privilege as a White, straight, cisgender female. I didn't recognize the advantages of living in a safe environment and having access to education and resources.

I remember one of my classmates in graduate school saying, "You can't pull yourself up by your bootstraps if you don't have any boots." I think about that statement all the time. So often, we neglect to consider that everyone starts from a different place. We blame their lack of progress or accomplishments on their lack of hustle. However, the reality is that many people in society have faced barriers that others have not had to contend with, such as racial discrimination, lack of financial resources, inadequate family support and guidance, and adverse childhood experiences. Perhaps this is the case for you as well.

Unfortunately, your inner critic doesn't care that the playing field isn't level. It doesn't take into account the impact of your environment or your lack of access to privilege. Your inner critic will still scold you for performing poorly on an exam without considering how difficult it is for you to concentrate when you are worried about shielding your siblings from an abusive parent. It will still be tough on you for being late to work while failing to acknowledge that you can't afford to fix your car and the bus is unreliable. It will still beat you up for not getting that promotion at work without stopping to consider that people of your gender (or race, religion, class, sexual orientation, etc.) are held to a higher standard in your organization and have to work harder than the "bro" down the hall.

If your inner critic is constantly saying cruel things to you and making you feel like you're not doing enough, consider the bigger picture. Perhaps your roommate got into grad school easily, but she didn't have to deal with the aftermath of a sexual assault. Perhaps your friend is effortlessly training for a 5k, but he doesn't have a diagnosis of depression to contend with. Remember that there are real societal, economic, and environmental barriers that individuals must work to overcome, yourself included. Fighting against those barriers makes you a warrior. Give yourself credit for everything you do in the face of adversity.

Capitalism Loves Your Inner Critic

Capitalism is more than happy to encourage your inner critic to keep doing its dirty work. There is some serious money to be made when you don't like yourself. You don't look like a model or celebrity? Buy this eyeshadow kit or "miracle" foundation. Your house doesn't look like an HGTV model home? Get your ass to a home improvement store for the latest line of organizational products and decor. Companies have a vested interest in you feeling like you are broken and need to change so that you buy their products to "fix" yourself. But you were never broken to begin with.

One of the biggest lies that we have been told by capitalism is that thin equals healthy. I was 40 years old before I finally caught on to the lies of diet culture and became aware that bodies of all sizes can be healthy. I don't want you to wait as long as I did to internalize that message. I was at a Lizzo concert a few weekends ago and saw bodies of *all* sizes on stage singing, dancing, twerking, and playing musical instruments for two hours. If that's not fitness and health, I don't know what is. Although companies want you to aspire to images of thinness and fitness that are not real or attainable, anyone can be healthy, regardless of their size, if they eat a decent amount of plants, move their body, avoid smoking, and limit alcohol. You also need to remember that if we all ate the same foods and followed the same workout routine, we would still have different bodies. Embrace body diversity.

Let's stop believing capitalism's lie that you are flawed and that you need to spend a large sum of money "fixing" yourself. Rather, devote that time, energy, and money to something meaningful (like donating to Planned Parenthood!). Instead of trying to reduce your body fat to some arbitrary percentage or making your house look like the pages of *Architectural Digest*, why not spend that time being awesome, discovering your identity, and dismantling systems of oppression?

Common Negative Thought Patterns

Your inner critic is so skilled at spouting off automatic negative thoughts that you often don't notice them popping into your head until you allow yourself to slow down, breathe, and reflect. Common negative thoughts often sound like these:

- I'm not good enough.
- I can't do anything right.
- If it's not perfect, I've failed.
- I should be perfect.
- I'm not working hard enough.
- I should be more (thin, intelligent, extroverted, motivated, put-together, etc.).
- I'm ugly.
- I can't let anyone down.
- I have to be strong.

- I should be in control all the time.

- I need everyone to like me.

We tend to accept what our inner critics say as true and accurate, but our minds aren't always right. The brain can make faulty connections and assumptions called *cognitive distortions*. Although everyone falls into these thought ruts occasionally, unchecked cognitive distortions can contribute to symptoms of anxiety and depression. Your thoughts matter. Thoughts become words, words become actions, and actions become habits, so it's essential to become aware of these thinking patterns. With practice, you can then become better at identifying and challenging these unhelpful thoughts. Here are some of the most common cognitive distortions that people struggle with. See if you can identify yourself in any of these examples.

Catastrophizing

Catastrophizing occurs when your brain leaps to the worst possible outcome in a situation, even if it is very unlikely to occur. You essentially make everything out to be a catastrophe. For example, if you feel nervous about riding a roller coaster, your inner critic might ask, *What if your seatbelt comes undone?* or *What if the car goes off the track?* Gee, thanks, inner critic, for making me imagine my potential demise at the county fair in front of the funnel cake stand. Catastrophizing blurs the difference between what's possible and what's probable. Is it possible that you could fly off a roller coaster and come crashing down on the lemonade stand? Yeah, it's possible. But is it probable? Definitely not. Thousands of people ride roller coasters every day and are perfectly fine. The most likely negative outcome is that you'll barf up your nachos, which is not ideal, but you'd survive.

All-or-Nothing Thinking

All-or-nothing thinking, also known as polarized thinking or black-and-white thinking, occurs when you view things in extremes. For example, if you are late to work because the metro is running behind, you consider your day wholly ruined. Or if you give a talk at work and stumble over one word, you believe that the entire presentation was an abject failure. When you think in all-or-nothing terms, you believe that things in life are either all good or all bad. The truth is that life is rarely so black and white. You can face something challenging but have an overall good day. You can make a mistake without your entire performance being a disaster. You can allow joy, gratitude, and fun to coexist with pain, frustration, and disappointment.

Emotional Reasoning

Emotional reasoning happens when you treat your emotions as facts. This type of thinking pattern assumes that your emotions are an accurate depiction of reality. You basically tell yourself, *I feel this way, so it must be true.* I engage in emotional reasoning every time I go down to the basement to turn off the lights at night. My brain tries to tell me there is a bogeyman downstairs that is going to get me if I don't hustle up the stairs as fast as possible after shutting off the lights. Once I reach the kitchen, that imaginary bogeyman disappears. Just because I felt that momentary fear in my basement did not mean that I was actually in danger.

The Fallacy of Fairness

The fallacy of fairness is the belief that everything in life should be fair and equal, which causes resentment when things don't go your way. When you have a specific view of what is and isn't fair, you may also impose certain standards on your partners, friends, and family. Let's say you enjoy picking out thoughtful gifts for your friends on birthdays.

You spend hours searching for the perfect present that you beautifully wrap for your loved one's big day. When your birthday comes around, you expect your friends to do the same for you. You feel hurt and let down when you don't receive a pile of beautifully wrapped gifts. However, your friends may simply express their affection differently than you. Perhaps they are more into planning dinners and fun activities to celebrate birthdays.

The Heaven's Reward Fallacy

The heaven's reward fallacy presumes that your self-sacrifice and hard work should bring about reward. Unfortunately, life isn't fair even if you work diligently to be a good person and do everything right. You can volunteer at the animal shelter, tip your local barista well, go above and beyond at work, finish your taxes on time, be a good listener to all your friends, and *still* end up with a parent diagnosed with cancer. Being good does not protect you from facing adversity.

Personalization

Personalization involves taking things personally even when they have nothing to do with you at all. Your brain essentially defaults to "What did I do?" or "I did something wrong" when things go awry. May I offer you a tiny truth bomb? It's not always about you. If you don't get that job offer or your crush doesn't call you to go out on a second date, it's not necessarily your fault. The company could have decided they didn't have the budget for the position. Or your date may have realized that they are not over their ex. You can't discount the other factors that could have contributed to the situation.

Overgeneralization

Overgeneralization occurs when you draw a faulty conclusion based on one small piece of information and apply it across the board to all future events. For example, if you trip and fall on your face in the club while wearing a new pair of Balenciaga shoes and, from that point forward, call yourself "clumsy," that would be overgeneralizing. Everyone falls on their ass at some point. That doesn't make you a klutz, but it does make you human.

Blaming

Blaming occurs when you hold everything and everyone, other than yourself, responsible when something goes wrong or when you feel emotional pain. A client of mine, Allison, half-assed a presentation at work. Rather than admit she didn't prepare well, she claimed her supervisors hadn't outlined the project expectations clearly enough. Blaming can also occur when *you* take the blame for anything and everything. Forest fires in California? You are responsible because you once drank out of a Styrofoam cup and contributed to climate change. Boss is in a mood? It must be your fault because you brewed hazelnut coffee this morning instead of French vanilla.

Being Right

Hello, all you know-it-alls out there! This one is for you if you feel compelled to be right *all the time*. With this cognitive distortion, you will go to any length to prove that your opinions and decisions are correct. We all have that one friend who is so insistent upon being right that they will interrupt a lovely dinner to google statistics or do a deep dive into their text messages from 2019 to prove their point rather than let it go. The problem with this way of thinking is that your relationships can become compromised when your focus is on being right instead of considering the other person's perspective or listening to them with respect. Your brain will trick you into believing that winning the argument is more important than the relationship.

The Fallacy of Control

The fallacy of control can operate in two different ways. On one end of the spectrum, you might believe that nothing is in your control and that you don't have agency over anything. This can lead you to feel helpless and assume a victim mentality. For example, if you felt so in over your head during your first semester in college, you might have stopped bothering to turn in any assignments at all. On the other end of the spectrum, you might feel responsible for everything and everyone. For example, suppose your partner is upset because they had a tough day. In that case, you feel accountable for cheering them up and making them happy. Or let's say your mom invites you to dinner and you'd prefer not to go, but you say yes anyway because you don't want her to feel disappointed. In reality, there are always things that will be both out of and within our control. Either way, you are not responsible for someone else's thoughts, emotions, and behaviors.

Jumping to Conclusions

Jumping to conclusions involves making assumptions that are not supported by evidence. There are two different forms of jumping to conclusions: mind reading and fortune telling. With mind reading, you assume you know what someone else is thinking. For example, you might go out to dinner with a group of friends and one particular friend seems off. In response, you immediately assume you did something to make your friend mad, even though there are a thousand different reasons why they might be distant or withdrawn. Their cat might be sick, or they might be facing downsizing at their job. You'll only know by talking with your friend directly.

Another way people often jump to conclusions is by fortune telling, which involves making predictions about the future based on limited information. For example, you might believe that you will never advance in your career just because you happened to be passed up for a promotion this year. No one can predict the future, but you can focus on taking control of the present.

When you find yourself making assumptions, ask yourself if your beliefs are supported by the facts. I once had a terrifying boss (whom I eventually came to adore) named Janice. Janice did not mess around. One time, I was meeting with her, and she asked about some fundraising statistics. I began my sentence with "Well, I assume . . ." and Janice immediately corrected me. She said, "Don't assume. You have to know!" That has been burned into my brain ever since.

Mental Filtering

Mental filtering involves dwelling on the negative aspects of a situation while tuning out the positive. Let's say you are feeling yourself as you arrive at a family event. Your hair is perfection, and your outfit is on point. You just posted a selfie on Instagram, and your friends love everything about your look. But then you run into your Aunt Geraldine, a salty old broad from Brooklyn. And she says snidely, "That outfit is interesting." Intellectually, you know that you shouldn't care about what Aunt Geraldine says or thinks, but you immediately feel deflated. This is your brain filtering out all the positive feedback and only giving weight to the negative feedback.

How to Reframe Negative Thoughts

It's important to learn how to rein in your inner critic and reframe negative thinking patterns because your thoughts, feelings, and behaviors are connected. What you think influences how you feel, and how you feel affects what you do—and vice versa. That means one negative thought can trigger a chain reaction of emotions and actions.

Let's say I screw up and forget to update my calendar about an upcoming coffee date with a friend. The day comes and my friend calls me wondering where the heck I am. My first thought might be *I am such an idiot!* (overgeneralization) or *I can't get anything right* (all-or-nothing thinking). I feel embarrassed that I forgot the appointment, guilty for letting my friend down, and disappointed that I am missing out on a pumpkin spice latte. I'm in a giant spiral of negativity. Because I feel so bad, I skip my daily walk and feel distracted for a couple of hours. Then I feel even worse because I don't do anything I had planned, like making progress on a writing project and putting away laundry.

Now let's look at the same situation but see how things might turn out differently if I challenge my negative thoughts instead. After realizing that I blanked on the coffee date, I could tell myself, *Hey, this sucks, but everyone makes mistakes*, and *I am human and doing the best I can*. I may still feel disappointed that I forgot the meetup with my friend, but I am not sinking into a shame spiral. Giving myself some grace allows me to have the courage to apologize to my friend for my error, reschedule for another time, and carry on with the rest of my day. It also allows me to tune in and ask myself, without judgment, what contributed to my error and what I might need at that moment. Maybe I'm not getting enough sleep and need to take something off my plate. Shifting negative thoughts gives me a chance to learn from the experience.

Many people think they need their inner critic to be productive and successful. They fear that if they rein in their inner critic, they will feel unmotivated and lazy. But that tends to not be the case. Think about it this way. Let's say you decide to hire a personal trainer to train for a 5k race. One trainer never lets you have a rest day, makes you work out to the point of exhaustion, and constantly calls you names. Another trainer gives you rest days, designs your workouts to be appropriate for your level of ability, and is really encouraging. Which trainer do you think will provide you with better results? Most likely, the latter. It's the same with your inner critic. When that voice in your head is really harsh, it brings you down and holds you back.

Reframing takes some practice, and it can feel awkward at first. But there are several strategies that can help you get there, which I'll outline in the rest of this chapter. Ultimately, you get to decide which thoughts to keep and which to let go of. I like to think of the mind as a garden. You nurture and grow the flowers, vegetables, and fruit (your beneficial and realistic thoughts) and discard the weeds (your unhelpful and untrue thoughts) before they overtake your garden.

Put Your Thoughts on Trial

One way to reframe your negative thoughts into something more helpful or realistic is to put your thoughts on trial, as if you are a lawyer. In fact, going to law school is something I briefly considered after graduating college. Although I didn't honestly want to be a lawyer, I had watched *Legally Blonde* and wondered if I could get into a law program like Elle Woods. I fantasized about wearing a killer suit and designer heels while grilling some dirtbag on the stand. In reality, law was not the right career for me since I try to see and empathize with all sides of a situation. I want everyone to win!

But even though I'm not an attorney living out dramatic scenes in the courtroom, I regularly put Nelson and my negative thoughts on trial. You do not have to accept your thoughts at face value. Here are a few questions to help you cross-examine those unhelpful cognitions:

- Is this thought actually true?

- Is there any evidence to support the validity of this thought?

- Is there another way to look at this situation?

- What would you say to a friend with a similar thought?

- Are there any cognitive distortions impacting your thinking?

- Do you have unreasonable expectations for yourself? Are you holding yourself to an impossible standard?

- What else could have contributed to how you are feeling or to your current situation?

- How can you reframe this thought to be more helpful or kind?

- Are you thinking in absolutes (e.g., using words like *always* or *never*)?

Here are a few examples of what reframing can look like when you put your thoughts on trial:

OLD THOUGHT: I will never be able to run a 5k. I'm not athletic.

NEW THOUGHT: If I keep trying, I can work up to a 5k. Just because I never played sports doesn't mean that I can't be fit.

OLD THOUGHT: I'm going to blow this presentation at work. I'm not good at public speaking.

NEW THOUGHT: Public speaking doesn't come easy to me. Still, I know this material well, and I can ask my colleagues to help me practice my presentation.

OLD THOUGHT: I look awful. I feel ugly.

NEW THOUGHT: It can be hard to shake off society's expectations for attractiveness. I am my own worst critic. What I look like and weigh are the least intriguing things about me. I can focus on what I like about myself and find an outfit I feel confident in. I can unfollow people who make me feel bad about myself on social media.

Remember that thoughts don't have any intrinsic meaning or value. You don't have to feed into a negative thought or be defined by it. You can find a more balanced and realistic way of thinking by making your negative and irrational thoughts take the stand. I rest my case!

Use the Power of Positive Self-Talk

Another strategy for taming your inner critic and managing negative thoughts is to practice positive self-talk and affirmations. I know some of you might be rolling your eyes right now and thinking, *Ugh, here comes the part where the overly cheery therapist tells me to think happy thoughts.* I hear you. Positive self-talk sometimes conjures up Al Franken's character, Stuart Smalley, in the *Saturday Night Live* skit from the '90s. Stuart gazes at himself in the mirror and says, "I'm good enough, I'm smart enough, and doggone it, people like me!"

My goal is not for you to tell yourself a bunch of inspirational quotes that you don't believe so you can join the "good vibes only" club. My goal is for you to start countering your negative thoughts with something realistic and beneficial. Positive affirmations provide a new script for your brain so you can respond to the world more effectively. For example, if you often think, *I never do anything right*, then you will likely feel insecure and shy away from trying new things. But if you can shift that thought to *I will do my best and learn from my mistakes*, then you will likely feel hopeful and curious about taking on new challenges.

It's tough to eliminate all negative thoughts, thanks to the negativity bias I discussed earlier in the chapter, but here are some examples of positive affirmations that can help you cope with challenging situations:

- I can do challenging things.

- I am doing my best, and my best is good enough.

- I am stronger than I think.

- I have conquered challenges before, and I can do it again.

- I'm not perfect. I am human.

- Making mistakes is how I learn and grow.

- Progress is more important than perfection.

- The right opportunities will unfold at the right time for me.

- Not everyone has to like me.

- I am both enough just as I am and a work in progress.

- It's okay to prioritize my mental, emotional, and physical needs.

- Everyone is on a different path.

- Rest is essential and not something that has to be earned.

- Taking care of myself enables me to give to others.

- I trust my inherent wisdom.

Pay attention to the things around you that you find inspiring. Quotes from movies, books, or spiritual texts can be a source of inspiring affirmations. You might also identify lyrics from your favorite songs that can become personal mantras. For example, Snoop Dogg has an incredibly catchy tune, "The Affirmations Song," that features lyrics like "I believe in myself" and "Every problem has an answer." If you need a quick boost or an easy way to practice positive self-talk, check it out. I'm seriously making this song a permanent part of my morning routine. Thank you, Snoop!

When you find some affirmations that resonate with you, write them out and post them in places where you'll see them often. For example, I wear bracelets with mantras on them and put quotes on my corkboard to see them while I am working. It can take some time to internalize this new way of talking to yourself, especially if you have a tendency toward perfectionism, grew up in a critical environment, or have experienced trauma, so writing out these affirmations can serve as a helpful reminder when you need it most.

Get Out There and Suck at Something

It's incredibly common for inner critics to uphold an impossible standard of perfection. That's because the allure of perfectionism is seductive. It leads you to fool yourself into thinking that if you do everything right, plan for every possible scenario, and look immaculate, nothing terrible will happen. You believe that you will be able to shield yourself from pain or prevent being disliked if you are "perfect." Simply put, perfectionism makes you think you can control the uncontrollable in an uncertain world. Unfortunately, it's not feasible to plan for every possible outcome. And some people may never like you even though you have the best intentions.

Fortunately, an antidote to perfectionism is to get out there and intentionally go suck at something. Be willing to be imperfect. Taking an improv acting class was one of the best things I ever did for myself. I am an introvert and was leery of acting silly in front of others for fear of being judged. But I learned to trust my class and fellow improv actors. They wouldn't think poorly of me if I botched a scene or did something off the wall. In improv class, there is no "right" or "perfect" way to create a story with someone. The chance to make mistakes and experience new ways of being in a safe setting was a remarkable experience.

There are several ways you can give something new and unfamiliar a try. Today I tried two new hairstyles that I saw on Pinterest. I looked like a pioneer woman on the Oregon Trail, but that's okay. A friend of mine goes to pottery class, and her creations often accidentally resemble female genitalia. No big deal. She can still use them as badass flower vases.

Experience this for yourself. If you are tone-deaf, go sing some karaoke and own it. If you can't cook, give a recipe a try and forgive yourself when you overcook the chicken or substitute salt for sugar in the cake. Allow yourself to be imperfect so you can learn that the world won't fall apart if you make a mistake. Once your brain understands that mistakes or failures are opportunities for growth and learning, you will be unstoppable.

Overcome Weird and Scary Shit in Your Brain (a.k.a. Intrusive Thoughts)

Intrusive thoughts are distressing and unwanted thoughts that pop into your head seemingly out of nowhere. The content of these thoughts is often strange or embarrassing, and it can involve themes of germs or contamination, violence or aggression, religion or morality, devious sexual acts, or other shocking behavior done in a public setting. Although these thoughts can be unsettling, nearly everyone has intrusive thoughts from time to time.

The other day, I took my kids to the Cheesecake Factory in the Tysons Corner Galleria, this gigantic, bougie mall outside of Washington, DC. We were on the second level, and I could look down at the floor below me. Suddenly, I thought, *What if I ran and jumped over the guard rail like Spiderman?* This was not a suicidal thought, nor did I have any desire to harm myself. I was way too excited about the prospect of having a bread basket in front of me momentarily. I knew this was just my brain scanning my environment for potential danger. So I told my brain, *Okay, brain, quit being weird. You and I both know I will carefully use the escalator.*

Intrusive thoughts are harmless if they occur occasionally, and they are usually not indicative of any deep meaning. You are not compelled to ruminate or act on them. You also do not need to feel ashamed of them. If you notice occasional intrusive thoughts, remind yourself that the human brain has strange thoughts sometimes and that following or investigating these thoughts isn't necessary. It can also be beneficial to use grounding techniques (chapter 3) or to engage in a distraction technique for a few minutes. If intrusive thoughts become more intense or start interfering with your everyday life, don't hesitate to contact a mental health professional for support. This could be an indication that these thoughts are symptoms of trauma or another mental health condition.

Break the Vicious Cycle of Overthinking

When you have an overactive inner critic, it can lead to a vicious cycle of overthinking. My inner critic, Nelson, used to make me overthink all the time. At my first office job in Washington, DC, I was tasked with sending out the office holiday cards. There were literally thousands of cards that I needed to send out. This was a massive project that involved making all the address updates, adding my coworkers' contact information, inserting the cards into envelopes, and sealing and stamping each one. Could I do this project on my own? No. Did I ask for the help I needed on this project? Also no, because my inner critic was a jerk. The dialogue in my head went a little something like this:

> LIZ: Holy shit, I will not be able to get this done in time. I should ask for help.

> NELSON: No way, figure this out on your own. If you ask for help, your boss will think you can't do your job.

> LIZ: But at this rate, it's going to be New Year's Eve before these get into the mail!

> NELSON: If you stay late and come in early, you can do it yourself.

> LIZ: But this is a lot. Shouldn't I ask for a hand? Maybe someone knows an easier way to do this.

> NELSON: No way! People will think you are a failure. You should be able to handle it!

> LIZ: Maybe you're right. If I can't handle a simple project like sending out holiday cards, my boss will think I can't do my

job. I'll never get promoted if my boss believes I can't do my job. Or even worse, I could get fired. And if I get fired, I won't be able to pay my rent. If I can't pay my rent, my roommate will hate me. Better suck it up and do this thing. On second thought, maybe I should leave work early and meet my friends for happy hour at Capitol Lounge for wings and beer. I'll worry about this project later.

NELSON: Yeah, that sounds like a good plan.

(Cut to me sending out the final cards on New Year's Eve. Oops.)

As you can see, overthinking leads to stress, worry, rumination, and procrastination. Fortunately, you can take a few steps to break the vicious cycle:

Step 1: Recognize and acknowledge your thoughts.
The first step in breaking the cycle of overthinking is to notice the thoughts going through your mind without judging them or reacting to them in any way. Simply pause to acknowledge these thoughts for what they are. They are simply thoughts. They are not facts, and they do not hold any special power over you. When you begin pausing and noticing in this manner, it can help you unhook from strong thoughts that try to take over.

Step 2: Avoid turning to social media for additional information or distraction.
When overthinking sets in, it's common to seek a distraction or try to gain more information. You might be tempted to scroll on Instagram, watch TikTok videos for hours, or endlessly research solutions for whatever challenge you are facing. But distracting yourself only compounds your stress, and excessive research can lead to analysis paralysis, making it even harder for you to make decisions.

Step 3: Breathe, pause, and ground yourself in the present moment.

When your thoughts feel overwhelming, it's tempting to want to do something immediately and respond reactively. Resist that urge and give yourself permission to pause for a moment. Breathe so your nervous system can regulate itself and get out of "fight, flight, freeze, or fawn" mode. (More on this in the next chapter.) Use your senses to focus your attention on the present moment and whatever you notice in your environment.

Step 4: Switch up your environment and seek a new perspective.

Take a moment to step outside and walk around the block. Grab a glass of water, or give yourself a few minutes to stretch, play with your dog, or do something creative. A small change in scenery can help you see your situation differently.

Step 5: Take a tiny step toward action.

Thoughtful action can be an effective antidote when your thoughts feel overwhelming. Ask yourself what might help you feel 5 percent less overwhelmed. What might make you feel a little bit better? This could be asking for help from a trusted friend or colleague. You could write down the top three things that would make your day feel productive or meaningful. Taking action could also look like sitting with your discomfort while you take the first step on a difficult task you've been avoiding. You can set a timer and spend 5 or 10 minutes tackling that annoying project.

Step 6: Be patient with yourself and practice self-compassion.

Everyone gets overwhelmed sometimes and overthinks situations. You are not alone! Remind yourself that this is hard, but you will figure it out. Ask yourself what it is that you genuinely need. (Consider revisiting the earlier chapter on self-care.) Maybe you could benefit from going to bed early or eating more regular meals. You may need to summon the courage to ask for some support. You may also need to develop some self-compassion by treating yourself like you would a good friend, which takes me to my next point.

Develop Self-Compassion

I'm willing to bet that you grew up hearing about the importance of self-esteem. While a healthy sense of self-esteem can help you achieve your goals, the problem is that self-esteem is often connected to external achievements, like getting a promotion, earning a high salary, conquering some athletic feat, or looking a certain way. This makes self-esteem challenging to sustain because whenever you experience a setback, your self-esteem takes a hit. Self-esteem can also set you up for failure because there will always be someone more attractive, powerful, wealthier, or talented than you. As Theodore Roosevelt is thought to have said, "Comparison is the thief of joy." Teddy makes a solid point. When you compare yourself to others, you feel dissatisfied and deflated.

So what's a person to do? The answer is to develop self-compassion. I was an adult working in the mental health field when I first heard of this concept, and let me tell you, it's a game changer, friends. In contrast to self-esteem, self-compassion is not tied to your achievements. Rather, it's the practice of treating yourself with kindness in spite of your shortcomings, failures, and mistakes. This doesn't mean you give yourself a free pass to screw up without caring. It means that you treat yourself kindly and fairly in the wake of challenges so that you can learn and grow rather than get defeated or stuck in a shame spiral. Basically, self-compassion acknowledges that you are a perfectly imperfect human, just like everyone else. Refreshing, right?

In order to start fighting back against your inner critic with a dose of self-compassion, try asking yourself what advice you would give to a friend going through the same situation or having the same thought. Often, we are much kinder to our friends than to ourselves. Treat yourself like you would a cherished and respected friend. Don't let your inner critic say anything to you that you wouldn't say to someone you love.

One of my clients, Abby, was hoping to get into a mentoring program offered by her workplace. She thought she had done well interviewing for the program, but unfortunately, she was not selected. Her first instinct was to ask herself, *What's wrong with me? Clearly, I'm not good enough.* She blamed herself for not spending more time on the application and reviewing interview questions. Abby felt down about herself and angry.

But then Abby took some time to reflect and ask herself what advice she would give her best friend in the same situation. She told herself that this application was a new experience and that she did the best she could given that she didn't have a full picture of what admittance to this program would require. In turn, Abby recognized that getting into this program was not connected to her worth as a person or her talents or abilities. Abby identified that she had too many activities and social obligations on her plate that made it hard for her to prioritize the program application. She needed to start saying no to commitments that weren't aligned with her goals and values. She also realized that having additional work experience would put her in an even better position to apply again next year. Practicing self-compassion allowed Abby to feel content with herself and learn from her experiences.

Give Your Inner Critic a Name

As I mentioned at the beginning of this chapter, I gave my inner critic a name to make it easier to talk back to any source of negativity in my head. I encourage you to do the same. Name your inner critic whatever you want—Harold, Thelma, The Jerk in My Head. Anything goes. Naming your inner critic is helpful because it creates space between you and your negative thoughts. It diffuses negative thinking and takes away some of that thought's power over you. My internal conversations with Nelson these days look a little different now that I challenge my unhelpful thoughts and practice self-compassion:

Meeting on a Zoom call:

> NELSON: Your neck looks weird.
>
> LIZ: Seriously, Nelson? My neck looks weird?
>
> NELSON: Yeah, maybe you should have worn some makeup or earrings or something.
>
> LIZ: Whatever, Nelson. I look great. No one looks fantastic on a video call. Stop being a dick!
>
> *(Cut to me feeling totally fine about myself and my appearance.)*

Trying to write this book:

> NELSON: What do you think you're doing?
>
> LIZ: Writing a book on mental health.
>
> NELSON: Are you serious?
>
> LIZ: Um . . . yeah. Yes, I am serious.
>
> NELSON: But you don't know anything! No one wants to hear what you have to say. You don't even have a doctorate. A lot of people know way more than you do.
>
> LIZ: I don't know everything, but I know some things. And maybe someone will find this book helpful.
>
> NELSON: Okay, then. Fine.
>
> *(Cut to me continuing to write this book.)*

Going for a 20-minute walk:

NELSON: That wasn't a long enough workout. You should do more.

LIZ: Whatever, dude. I just walked a mile.

NELSON: You should have done two miles.

LIZ: Stop being a jerk, Nelson. Any physical activity is better than no physical activity. Plus, I feel better after my walk than I did before. And I spent time outside, away from my desk.

(Cut to me continuing to try to fit in physical activity whenever possible.)

Nelson is no longer running the show. When he pipes up, I remind Nelson that I am human and doing my best. You may have an inner critic, but you also have a wise, guiding voice. That's your authentic self. You can more easily listen to your inner wisdom by quieting your inner critic. Don't let that negative voice in your head hold you back.

Action Items

1. Think about the last time you made a mistake or something didn't go as planned. What automatic thoughts popped into your head?

2. After you identify those negative thoughts, reframe them into something more beneficial using any of the techniques from this chapter.

3. Come up with three positive statements you can use for daily affirmations. Write them or post them in a place where you will read them often.

THE MIND-BODY CONNECTION

 Feelings are just your body talking to you about how you're doing in the moment. Even if you've gotten used to ignoring them, they're still talking to you. Tune in to your breathing, and then your body, and then your emotions. It's a little thing that pays off big.

—Allyson Dinneen

Your Brain's Most Important Job

Our brains can do some incredibly complicated and amazing things. For example, my brain remembers all the lyrics to Britney Spears's song "Oops! . . . I Did It Again" from 2000 and keeps a running list of all the stuff I need from the grocery store. But as I discussed previously, the number one thing that our brains care about is keeping us safe. Our brains are hardwired to be on the lookout for danger. It's like our own personal 24-hour, seven-day-a-week, high-tech surveillance mechanism. This fine-tuned system ramps us up for action in response to any perceived threats and calms us down when the danger has passed.

Back in the days of the caveman, these threats involved life and death. Our earliest ancestors were constantly on the lookout for unhinged hippos or rivals trying to attack and steal the last of the berries. Even in our modern-day world, our brains are great at dealing with catastrophic threats with a clear end point. You can probably think of a time when you were about to cross a busy street and quickly jumped out of the way to narrowly avoid a speeding car. You didn't even have to think about taking action. Your brain automatically saved your behind. After the speeding car passed, you probably noticed that your heart was beating faster, you felt a bit jumpy, and you were breathing a little heavier than usual. But after a few minutes, you regained a sense of calm again.

The problem with the brain's surveillance system in our current world is that it can interpret events as dangerous even when they are not actual threats. Sometimes the threats we encounter in daily life are real, but sometimes they are imagined. And dangers in our modern world, like climate change and financial stress, don't typically have a clear end point. We want our brains to alert us when we need to get out of the way of a speeding car, but we don't want them to signal danger whenever our boss enters the room or Debbie has a stank face at book club.

The Upstairs and Downstairs Brains

To better understand that noggin of yours, it's helpful to think of your brain in two parts: the upstairs and the downstairs. The downstairs brain is responsible for controlling essential bodily functions, regulating emotions, and keeping you safe. This part of the brain houses the amygdala (the fear and emotion center), the hippocampus (the learning and memory center), and the brain stem, which regulates breathing, heart rate, and blood pressure.

The upstairs brain is in charge of higher-order processes, like critical thinking, problem-solving, decision-making, and planning. This part of the brain contains the prefrontal cortex (the executive functioning center). The prefrontal cortex is the last area of the brain to develop—it doesn't stop developing until your mid-20s—so for those of you in your teens or early 20s, there's no shame in getting guidance and feedback from people you trust. Your brain is still a work in progress.

The upstairs and downstairs brains must work together to share and process information, meaning that you need a strong ladder (or staircase) to connect the upstairs and downstairs. If these two areas are not integrated, you may react to stressful situations without stopping to think of the consequences of your actions. Can you think of a time when you felt overwhelmed, irritated, or angry, leading you to say or do something that you later regretted? Perhaps you flipped someone off when they cut you off in traffic or punched a wall in high school when you got mad at your best friend. This reactivity happened because your downstairs brain took the wheel in the face of stress, causing your upstairs brain (your rational, thinking side) to take a back seat. Neuropsychiatrist Dr. Daniel Siegel calls this process "flipping your lid."

Part of the reason you flip your lid has to do with your personal surveillance system, which is constantly on the lookout for danger. This surveillance system, known more formally as the autonomic nervous system, receives messages from your downstairs brain whenever the amygdala detects a threat in your environment. Your autonomic nervous system then mobilizes your body to prepare it for action against the potential threat.

The autonomic nervous system can be divided into two parts: the sympathetic nervous system and the parasympathetic nervous system. Just like you need your upstairs and downstairs brains to work together, you also need the sympathetic and parasympathetic nervous systems to collaborate. As you go about your day, these two systems work together to maintain a sense of balance.

The Sympathetic Nervous System

The sympathetic nervous system governs your acute stress response, and it gets activated whenever you sense a threat in your environment.

Importantly, your brain can perceive both physical and psychological threats as life-threatening. A physical threat pertains to your physical safety, while a psychological threat impacts your emotional and mental well-being:

- **Physical threat:** You are hiking at the Grand Canyon and decide to get a picture right at the edge of the gorge. As you are posing, you slip on the gravel beneath you. At the last second, you grab a branch and save yourself from plunging thousands of feet to the ground below. Crisis averted! (Also, please be careful taking selfies next to cliffs, okay?)

- **Psychological threat:** Your boss asks you to give a big client presentation at work. You are new to public speaking, and this is an important client that your organization can't afford to lose. Your thoughts start to spiral, and you wonder what would happen if you were to botch this project. You begin having difficulty focusing and concentrating because of your anxiety about the presentation.

In both situations, your brain responds as if you are in serious danger (even though only one of these threats is life-threatening) by triggering the release of stress hormones, like adrenaline and cortisol, into your body. As a result, your pupils dilate and your skin gets flushed. Your breathing becomes shallow and rapid so your lungs can increase their oxygen intake. Your muscles tense up in preparation for physical exertion. Your digestive system shuts down so your body can divert energy elsewhere. (This is why you get butterflies in your stomach when you are nervous. It's also why it's not a great idea to eat a grande burrito supreme before a nerve-racking presentation.) Your mind goes blank and you have trouble focusing, or you become irritable and on edge.

I imagine this happened to many of us in middle school when we encountered our crushes and forgot what we had planned to say. I still remember being thrilled that my fifth-grade crush, Chad, and I were in the same art class. Chad was the best dressed out of all the elementary school kids. His mom took him to the big mall an hour away while the rest of us went back-to-school shopping at Farm King and Sears. I had visions of Chad and me bonding over our shared love of collages constructed with torn-up *Good Housekeeping* magazines. But since I froze every time I saw him (and also happened to be sporting a mullet and thick Coke-bottle glasses), I only dared to talk to him once.

The freeze response that I had whenever I saw Chad represents one of the four reactions that you can have in response to real or perceived threats: You can lash out against the threat (fight), run away from it (flight), feel stuck and unable to move (freeze), or try to appease the source of the threat to avoid any conflict (fawn). You don't consciously choose these reactions—they just happen automatically.

The Fight Response

The fight response occurs when your sympathetic nervous system responds to threats with irritability, anger, or aggression. Almost every action movie has a scene where the main character has to defend themselves and a rumble ensues. My favorite fight scenes are between Daniel Cleaver and Mark Darcy in the *Bridget Jones's Diary* movies. Daniel makes an insensitive comment, the level-headed and buttoned-up Mark finally loses his cool (flips his lid, if you will), and punches are thrown.

While working on Capitol Hill in my early 20s, I often stayed at the office late and walked home in the dark. I should have called for a ride, but I was looking to save a few dollars to spend on wings and beer at the Capitol Lounge's weekly happy hour. As I began my walk one night, I noticed a man following me. Somehow my mild Midwestern self puffed up, walked to the entrance of the nearest apartment building pretending it was my own, and raised my voice loud enough to yell, "You better keep on walking!" Fortunately, the man did keep on walking and left me alone (with my pounding heart). I now realize that when I uncharacteristically raised my voice, it was my fight response kicking in.

The Flight Response

The flight response involves running away from the threat. Think about those gazelles on the savanna fleeing from a hungry lion. The faster the gazelle runs, the less likely it becomes tartare. It's the same for humans. If I hear a fight breaking out in a nearby alley, you can bet I will hustle in the opposite direction and get myself to safety.

The flight response in our modern world might also manifest as distraction or avoidance. Suppose I am stressed out by the thought of doing my taxes. In that case, I might run away from the problem by deep cleaning my refrigerator or spending an hour online shopping for Halloween costumes. I've had clients who were worried about finances delay opening their mail because they wanted to avoid facing the extent of their debt.

The Freeze Response

When I was eight years old, I thought I found a dead opossum in my backyard. This qualifies as big excitement for a child growing up in small-town Illinois. The opossum's tongue stuck out of its mouth as it lay on its back, and its little feet were sticking up straight in the air. It was gross. So, of course, I had to get my brother to check out what looked like a giant dead rat on a stump. By the time my brother and I had returned, the opossum was nowhere to be found! It had been playing dead, likely to avoid the attention of my neighbor's dog. The opossum had responded to danger by freezing.

During the freeze response, you stiffen in place and feel paralyzed. Sometimes victims of physical violence will respond this way at the time of their attack, causing them to feel shame that they did not fight back against their attacker or run away. But as I mentioned earlier, nervous system responses are not always within your control, especially during life-threatening and traumatic events. The brain's fear center takes over and does what it feels is best to keep you safe at that moment.

The Fawn Response

A fourth way of responding to danger is the fawn response, in which a victim attempts to appease the perpetrator of the threat. Fawning can look like being helpful, walking on eggshells, suppressing your emotions, or trying to make others happy to decrease the likelihood of becoming a target of abuse or violence. The fawn response often occurs in abuse situations, such as when a child seeks to please an explosive parent or when an individual attempts to avoid the wrath of a controlling or violent partner.

The fawn response can lead to codependency, which is characterized by an unhealthy dynamic between two individuals. In codependent relationships, one person gives to another at the expense of their own needs, identity, and self-worth. (More on codependency in chapter 5.) Fawning can also contribute to depression, self-criticism, self-harm, and physical symptoms such as pain, headaches, stomachaches, and chronic illness.

The Parasympathetic Nervous System

Now that you've learned how the sympathetic nervous system works, let's shift gears by talking about its counterpart: the parasympathetic nervous system. Known as your body's "rest and digest" system, the parasympathetic nervous system calms you down after the actual or perceived threat has passed. It's responsible for your restoration, growth, and repair.

One of the key players in the parasympathetic nervous system is the vagus nerve (pronounced like the city of Las Vegas), which is the longest cranial nerve in your body. You can think of it as the U.S. Highway 20 of your mind and body. The vagus nerve originates in the brain stem, runs through the face and throat, and continues all the way down into the abdomen. The vagus nerve oversees your mood, breathing, digestion, heart rate, and immune response. It may also play a role in the gut-brain axis I talked about in chapter 1.

Because the vagus nerve is key to managing your mood, anxiety, and stress response, stimulating this bundle of parasympathetic fibers can help restore a sense of safety in your mind and body. Toward the end of this chapter, you'll find some nervous system hacks that will allow you to tap into your vagus nerve and tap out of reactivity.

Trauma and the Nervous System

When I talk to my clients about the nervous system and its role in their well-being, I often discuss "getting back to the middle"—to that space between being ramped up versus shut down. Some mental health professionals refer to this as being in your window of tolerance, which refers to the place where you can manage the stressors of the everyday world without going into a tailspin. When you are in your window of tolerance, you feel safe, capable, and in control.

However, what often happens in our modern-day world is that our nervous systems get stuck. Many of my clients grew up in unpredictable, chaotic, and unsafe environments and now live their lives in a state of constant hyperarousal, meaning they're always in fight-or-flight mode. Others spend much of their time in a state of hypoarousal, meaning they feel distracted, frozen, and shut down. This is the effect of trauma on the nervous system.

Trauma is any distressing event that overwhelms an individual's ability to cope and takes away their sense of power or control. Trauma can occur anytime you fear for the physical, emotional, or psychological safety of yourself or someone you love. A traumatic event might be a single isolated incident, such as a car accident, or occur over a long period of time, such as childhood abuse or intimate partner violence. The cumulative impact of microaggressions, which are subtle acts of bias or discrimination toward an oppressed or targeted group, is also a cause of trauma. Finally, vicarious trauma occurs when a person, such as a first responder or health care worker, witnesses a traumatic event or has exposure to stressful situations.

After the experience of trauma, it can be difficult for the upstairs brain to be in charge. That's because trauma rewires your brain to be hypersensitive to threat, so your personal surveillance system perceives events as dangerous even when you are safe. You get pushed out of your window of tolerance more easily, causing you to feel shut down or stuck on high alert all the time. As Dr. Frank Anderson, a psychiatrist and trauma specialist, explains, "Trauma blocks love and connection."[4] In other words, the experience of trauma can inhibit your capacity to feel emotionally and physically safe with other people. This makes it difficult to trust others enough to be authentic and vulnerable, which are essential components of love and connection.

Although no two people respond to trauma the same way, here are some common symptoms you can experience after trauma:

- Difficulty concentrating or focusing
- Feelings of shame and low self-worth
- Difficulty trusting others
- Anxiety, panic attacks, and depression
- Headaches and chronic pain
- A feeling of disconnection from your body
- Numbness
- Difficulty sleeping
- Overwhelming emotions

- A lack of hope about the future

- A loss of motivation and direction

- Changes in how you view yourself, others, and the world

Your symptoms in the present may also be tied to the trauma experienced by previous generations, a concept called intergenerational or historical trauma. Although you may think that it's only possible to inherit your dad's old guitar or your grandmother's crystal vase, you can inherit more from previous generations than you think.

You Inherit More Than Just Your Grandma's Antique Dinnerware

Intergenerational trauma was first discussed in the context of Holocaust survivors and their families, but many circumstances have negative repercussions that span across generations. Your great-grandparents, grandparents, or parents may all have lived through the following:

- Poverty

- Discrimination and oppression

- Enslavement

- Living or fighting in war zones

- Forced migration

- Internment

- Religious indoctrination or involvement in cults

- Physical, verbal, or sexual abuse or interpersonal violence

- Incarceration or death of family members

- Worldwide pandemics

Intergenerational trauma can result in parenting challenges, difficulty trusting others, nightmares and sleep disturbances, anger and irritability, and difficulty making and maintaining relationships with others. I often see this dynamic in clients who are adult children of immigrants. They often feel a great deal of pressure to succeed (or have a lot of pressure placed on them) to make the sacrifices of their parents and grandparents worthwhile. These clients also often have difficulty setting healthy boundaries with their family of origin due to a sense of responsibility and obligation.

Unfortunately, previous generations have often learned to cope with trauma by minimizing or denying their experience. It isn't something that they talk about during Sunday dinner. They may not have been exposed to positive models of healthy communication or emotional expression because they had to prioritize survival. As a result, you may have no idea that your parents' or grandparents' way of behaving in the present is influenced by past adverse experiences.

The good news is that you can interrupt unhealthy patterns passed down across generations. Healing occurs when families dare to talk about secrets of the past and consider their impact on the present. Instead of defaulting to habitual ways of reacting, you can become mindful of substance and alcohol use, learn new parenting techniques, or seek therapy to improve your communication and emotional regulation skills. If you have been impacted by intergenerational trauma, you can also greatly benefit from the nervous system hacks detailed in the next section. Your healing goes beyond simply helping yourself. You are benefiting future generations.

Hack Your Nervous System

Now that you know how your brain and body work together, it's time to learn some techniques that activate the parasympathetic nervous system and stimulate the vagus nerve. The following activities all help your body get back into "rest and digest" mode. They promote calm, safety, healing, and restoration in your brain and body. Best of all, they don't cost a thing. (All yours for free!) Although these techniques won't remove the cause of your stress or fix all your problems, they can help your upstairs brain handle whatever life throws at you. They are all positive strategies for coping with challenges that don't lead to more stress in the long run.

Grounding Techniques

Grounding exercises help anchor (or "ground") you in the present moment when you feel overwhelmed, disconnected, or shut down. These strategies are particularly helpful if you're having flashbacks or intrusive thoughts. Often, grounding exercises involve using your five senses to stop ruminating about the past or worrying about the future—instead reorienting you to the present moment.

Some strategies work for some but not for others (you can find lots of suggestions online), so experiment and figure out which grounding techniques work for you. One of my favorite grounding exercises is called 5-4-3-2-1 and involves the following steps:

- Name five things you can see (e.g., pictures on the wall, your computer, your water bottle, your dog, your houseplant).

- Name four things you can feel (e.g., the chair beneath you, your feet on the floor, the feel of your clothes, the cool breeze of the air conditioner).

- Name three things you can hear (e.g., birds chirping, traffic, a phone ringing).

- Name two things you can smell (e.g., laundry detergent, someone cooking).

- Name one thing you can taste (e.g., toothpaste).

- Take a few deep breaths in and out.

Other grounding exercises include:

- Identifying items in the room for every color of the rainbow

- Naming all the towns and cities in your home state

- Trying to recite the lyrics of your favorite song

- Using all five senses to enjoy a snack or drink

- Slowly scanning your body from head to toe, noticing any sensations or tension in each part of your body

- Listening to music

Mindful Breathing

We have all heard the phrase "Just take a deep breath" when we're feeling upset or nervous. Mindful breathing can seem so simplistic. You may think it's something that only yogis do. However, science backs up the benefits of mindful breathing. Consciously slowing down your breathing—and in particular, making the exhale longer than the inhale—lowers your respiration rate, heart rate, and blood pressure and increases blood flow. Breathing literally brings you out of "fight, flight, freeze, or fawn" mode and back into "rest and digest" mode. As an added bonus, no one has to even know you are doing it.

There are many different breathing exercises out there, but here are a few that I often recommend to clients. If you mess up the counting, no big deal! It will still work as long as you focus on slowing down your breath. With all breathing exercises, stop if you feel lightheaded, dizzy, or agitated. It shouldn't feel like you are holding your breath. You should feel comfortable the entire time.

Square Breathing

Breathe in for four counts, hold for four counts, breathe out for four counts, and hold for four counts. Repeat as needed.

4-7-8 Breathing

Breathe in for four counts, hold for seven counts, and breathe out for eight counts. Repeat as needed.

Belly Breathing

Find a comfortable place to sit. Adjust your posture so you're sitting up straight (avoid slouching). Put one hand on your chest and one hand on your belly. Then breathe in and try to make your belly expand as you inhale. You want the hand on your stomach to rise as you inhale and drop back down as you exhale.

Alternate-Nostril Breathing

The basic premise of this exercise is to breathe in one nostril and breathe out of the other. Focusing on breathing in this specific way can help distract you from stressful or negative thoughts. Begin by sitting up nice and tall and taking a few deep breaths. When you're ready, bring your right hand up to your nose and block your right nostril with your thumb while breathing in through your left nostril. Then use your index finger to block your left nostril while you unblock and breathe out from the right nostril. With your left nostril still blocked, breathe in through the right nostril. Then block the right nostril with your thumb and breathe out through the left nostril. Repeat as needed for up to five minutes.

Pro tip: Practice these breathing techniques throughout the day, even if you feel relatively calm. This way, you will know what to do when challenging emotions surface.

Meditation

Meditation is a broad term for any practice that involves intentionally focusing your mind. I like to think of meditation as strength training for the brain. Most methods involve focusing your attention on the breath. When the mind wanders (and it definitely will!), gently bring yourself back to focusing on your breathing. As you meditate, your thoughts will come and go, but try not to engage with them.

The mistake I see most people make with meditation is that they try too much too soon and get frustrated. If you are interested in meditation, set a timer and try focusing on your breathing for just two minutes. Work your way up to longer stretches. You can also use a meditation app or search for some guided meditation scripts online. Meditation isn't about getting it "right" or doing it perfectly. It's about tuning in, clearing the distractions of daily life, and focusing your attention.

Visualization

Visualization is a mental exercise where you use your creativity to imagine your desired outcome for a particular situation. The point of visualization is to train your brain to think and feel a certain way. Athletes use visualization as part of their training for big competitions, but anyone can use this technique. When you visualize yourself taking action in response to your desired goal, you stimulate the same area of the brain that you would when performing the action in real life. It's like a mental dress rehearsal.

One key point of visualization is to not just picture the finish line. You also want to visualize yourself taking the steps involved in accomplishing your goal. For example, if you are a law student preparing for the bar exam, you can visualize the test day from start to finish. Imagine yourself waking up, getting ready, and heading to the test site. Picture yourself taking deep breaths and feeling calm, confident, and secure. See yourself answering the questions with ease as you complete the exam.

Progressive Muscle Relaxation

We often carry around tension in our muscles without realizing it. Progressive muscle relaxation is a type of guided meditation that involves systematically tensing and releasing different muscle groups in your body to let go of stress. It has been shown to lower blood pressure, ease migraines, and benefit sleep quality. You can find progressive muscle relaxation scripts and videos online or use a meditation app. Progressive muscle relaxation is a great way for releasing tension from the body for individuals who are unable to exercise due to injury or limited mobility.

Power Posing

Our body language says a lot about the state of our nervous system. When we feel successful, we take up space physically. For example, runners crossing the finish line after a difficult race raise their arms above their heads in a victory stance. When we feel proud, we stand up straight and tall with our chins lifted. Conversely, when we feel powerless, nervous, or insecure, we close ourselves off and make ourselves small. We might cross our arms in front of our chest or slump over with our eyes looking at the ground.

The good news is that posing in a powerful position, even when we aren't confident, can positively change how we feel and how we are perceived by others. As social psychologist Amy Cuddy explains in her TED Talk, "Your Body Language May Shape Who You Are," standing in a power pose for just two minutes can decrease the stress hormone cortisol (lowering stress) and increase testosterone (boosting confidence).

Try it out for yourself. Before an important job interview or presentation, strike a power pose in an empty bathroom stall to bolster your self-confidence. If you have wanted to speak up in a company-wide meeting for weeks, maintaining a confident stance can help you muster the courage to be part of the conversation. A power pose can look like raising your hands above your head in a victory stance, posing with your hands on your hips like Wonder Woman, or sitting confidently in your chair, allowing yourself to take up space.[5] (Just don't take up two chairs when there's a sweet little old lady standing next to you who would like to sit down.)

Being in Nature

Many of you know that being in nature is good for the soul. Not only does spending time outdoors lower stress levels, improve mood, and enhance mental clarity, but studies show that individuals who spend time in nature feel more satisfied with life.[6] What's more, being outdoors lends itself to disconnecting from your devices, which gives you a chance to decompress from sensory overload. You can instead take a moment to experience a sense of awe and wonder as you marvel at the beauty of the natural world.

You don't have to go hiking in the mountains or strolling through the forest to reap these benefits, especially if you live in an urban environment where these outdoor experiences aren't accessible to you. Even stepping outside for 10 minutes on your lunch break and taking a walk around the block can make a difference. Find green spaces near you, whether it's a local park, trail, or botanical garden.

Mindfulness

Mindfulness sometimes conjures up images of monks meditating on a mountaintop in Nepal, but anyone can practice mindfulness. It is not a religion, nor does it involve isolating yourself in solitude. Rather, mindfulness is about fully immersing yourself in a given task while using all of your senses to take in the experience. When you fully engage in the present moment, it gives your brain a break from replaying the past or worrying about the future.

Mindfulness does not have to be complicated or time-consuming. In fact, you can incorporate it into any activity that's already part of your routine. For example, you can mindfully wash the dishes, do laundry, or walk your dog. The point is to focus your full attention on the experience—feeling the suds of soap on your skin as you clean dishes, smelling the scent of lavender detergent as you fold laundry, or taking in the fresh air and warm sunshine as you walk your dog—instead of getting caught up in your thoughts.

Keeping busy with creative or engaging hobbies is another way to be mindful. Whether you're into knitting, coloring, playing sports, or cooking, these activities all offer an opportunity to flex your mindfulness skills instead of running on autopilot. Simply throw yourself into the experience. As an added benefit, hobbies are a great way to release tension and soothe your nervous system. One study found that making art reduces cortisol by 75 percent, even if the person had no prior art experience.[7]

Humming, Singing, Yawning, and Gargling

Have you ever belted out your favorite song at a concert or danced wildly in the living room while singing along to your favorite tunes? It feels good to sing—and singing is good for you too! Not only does it oxygenate your blood because of all the deep breathing involved, but it releases endorphins throughout your body, which are the brain's "happy" chemicals.

And when it comes to your nervous system, one of the simplest things you can do to bring about a sense of relaxation and calm is to sing. That's because the vagus nerve runs through the muscles in the back of your throat, so singing, humming, yawning, and gargling all activate the vagus nerve. Stop for a moment, take a deep breath in, and audibly sigh it out. See how you feel after!

Yoga Nidra

Yoga nidra is a restorative yoga practice that promotes a state of consciousness between wakefulness and sleep. When I do yoga nidra, I often feel like my mind is awake but my body is asleep. The practice helps you connect to your internal state, promotes meditative self-inquiry, and facilitates deep relaxation. Many guided audio and video recordings for yoga nidra are available online if you want to try it for yourself. Dr. Richard Miller, a psychologist and yogic scholar, is known for developing iRest, a guided meditation practice that combines yoga nidra with Western psychology and neuroscience. iRest has been shown to help individuals contending with chronic pain, posttraumatic stress disorder, depression, anxiety, and sleep issues.

Massage

That incredible feeling you get after a massage? That's your body in prime "rest and digest" mode. When you get a massage, it eases muscle tension, improves circulation, decreases blood pressure, and lowers heart rate—all of which promote relaxation. That means if you are looking for an excuse to book a massage and have room in your budget, do it!

That said, many of us don't have the financial resources for regular massages at the swanky local spa. (Three hundred dollars for an invigorating citrus aromatherapy massage? No, thanks, I'll save my money and sniff some candles at HomeGoods instead.) Getting a massage from another person can also be intimidating, especially if you have experienced previous trauma or sexual abuse.

Fortunately, it is possible to obtain the benefits of a massage at home by using your hands, a tennis or lacrosse ball, a foam roller, or other household items to give yourself a massage. Self-massage is free and accessible anytime you need it. You also know your body best and can target specific areas to release tension and boost circulation. There are self-massage and foam-rolling articles and instructional videos available online if you are interested in learning more.

Practicing Gratitude

It turns out that practicing gratitude isn't just a nostalgic Thanksgiving tradition—it can actually be good for your health! Several studies have shown that individuals who keep weekly or daily gratitude journals are more optimistic about the future, report fewer health problems, get better sleep, have more satisfying relationships, have stronger immune systems, and even have a decreased risk of heart attacks.[8] Importantly, gratitude is more than just looking on the bright side. It's about appreciating and making the most of what you have *now* instead of living in the past or the future.

Start small if you are having difficulty coming up with things for which you are grateful. For example, you can feel thankful for the little things in life, like your cup of coffee or the hot shower you took this morning. You could also feel thankful for your office bestie who makes work more fun, a fridge that is stocked with food, or the first daffodils that appear after a long winter. You might even feel thankful for catching the bus with a minute to spare. You can also have gratitude for more abstract or profound things, like staying in good health and keeping safe from harm.

There are many ways to express gratitude, such as keeping a gratitude journal, saving a gratitude list in the "notes" section of your phone, or writing down things you are thankful for on slips of paper and collecting them in a jar. You can also think of the people in your life who support you and make a point to let them know what you appreciate about them. When you express gratitude, it trains your brain to cope with adversity by reminding you of the meaning you have in your life.

Cold Water Immersion (a.k.a. the Diving Reflex)

Have you ever wondered why people find it helpful to splash cold water on their faces when they're feeling emotional? Or why so many people on social media are swearing by cold showers? It turns out that cold water stimulates the diving reflex, also known as the mammalian diving response, which is a quirky hack for feeling calmer. The diving reflex is a physiological response that occurs when you are submerged in cold water. Essentially, your body instinctually responds by slowing your heart rate and conserving oxygen to help you survive. That's your parasympathetic nervous system getting to work.

To stimulate the diving reflex, submerge your face in ice-cold water to your temples for as long as possible. Once you notice your heart rate slowing (or whenever you need to breathe), come back up for air. Since the nerves in your face connect to the vagus nerve, this hack can get your nervous system back into "rest and digest" mode. The shock of the cold water can also bring you back to the present moment. Once you feel calmer, you can more easily access that upstairs brain I talked about earlier. (If you have any health concerns, like heart issues, check with your doctor before trying this nervous system hack!)

Hugs, Cuddles, and Weighted Blankets

Hugs, cuddles, and weighted blankets all relax the nervous system through deep-pressure stimulation. More research is needed, but initial studies have shown that the deep-pressure stimulation from weighted blankets reduces anxiety symptoms, increases feel-good hormones (like oxytocin and serotonin), and decreases stress hormones (like cortisol).[9] Touch and gentle pressure can also evoke positive memories, like the memory of being snuggled as a toddler or held by someone you love. The physical sensation and firm pressure of a weighted blanket or hug can help you feel secure, safe, and grounded in the present moment.

This Is Your Brain on Booze

I can't have a chapter about the connection between the mind and body without spending time discussing the impact of alcohol on your brain. While any addictive substance can impact your mental health, I am choosing to focus on booze since "Big Alcohol" and their massive lobbying budgets downplay the addictive nature of this substance and treat it as harmless. They promote the message that if you are negatively impacted by alcohol, then *you* are the problem. That you lack willpower. But in reality, the substance is the problem, not you.

Before becoming a therapist, I worked as a fundraiser on Capitol Hill in Washington, DC. And there was alcohol everywhere. When things got stressful during campaign season, bottles of tequila and vodka would magically appear out of desk drawers and file cabinets. The office fridge always had beer along with stale pizza. I thought this was normal. In the world I was in, it was how everyone managed the extreme pressure they were under. I had superiors who I now realize were functioning alcoholics. They would pickle themselves in the evenings and somehow be back at work the following day. And I didn't know it at the time, but alcohol was making life harder for me too.

After a big night on the town in my 20s and 30s, I would experience what I called the "demons" the following day. The demons were an awful sense of sadness, despair, and anxiety. This is on top of what my friend Allie and I called the "DADS," which stood for the day-after-drinking shits—you know, those lovely gastrointestinal troubles that follow too many margaritas and 3:00 a.m. pizza. And, of course, headaches, nausea, and all the other awful stuff that comes with a hangover. I knew it was customary to feel physically awful after a boozy night out, but I didn't realize it also was common to feel like crap mentally. I thought it was just me. But it wasn't. "Hangxiety," or the anxiety you feel after drinking, is real. And I am going to give you the science behind it. I'm like Ms. Frizzle in an exceptional, grown-up version of *The Magic School Bus*. Buckle up, friends. You are in for an illuminating ride.

Imagine it's Friday at 5:30 p.m. after a stressful day at work, and you are finally at happy hour. It's a beautiful fall day, and you are drinking a glass of wine. Within 30 seconds, your stomach lining starts absorbing the alcohol. Within 5 minutes, alcohol reaches your brain. Within 10 minutes, you start to feel its effects as your brain begins releasing dopamine, which is associated with pleasure, and gamma-aminobutyric acid (GABA), which makes you feel calmer. Your inhibitions lower, your usual fears subside, and you feel more confident, meaning you can more easily talk to that attractive person at the bar. Work stress starts to melt away.

All is good, right? Not so fast. Your body is a finely tuned machine that seeks to maintain homeostasis and balance, so when your brain notices that flood of dopamine and GABA, it takes steps to counteract this artificial and elevated sense of pleasure and calm. It does so by releasing other chemicals, like glutamate, cortisol, and dynorphin, into your body. This is where the trouble starts. Glutamate is an excitatory transmitter that messes with your sleep and is responsible for those middle-of-the-night awakenings you experience after a boozy night out. Cortisol is a stress hormone that balances alcohol's depressant effect. Dynorphin, a natural sedative, brings you down and induces despair by preventing dopamine neurons from firing. This is probably why someone always ends up crying or mad at 2:00 a.m. after a night of drinking.

As the alcohol leaves your body, you experience feelings of withdrawal. You may have a pounding heart, difficulty breathing, low blood sugar, dehydration, and fatigue. You may also have uncertainty about what you said or did the night before. If you are trying to moderate your drinking, you may feel disappointed that you indulged more than you intended. You end up mad at yourself for wasting an entire day feeling hungover rather than spending the time doing something enjoyable or meaningful. All of these factors contribute to hangxiety.

This knowledge about alcohol might be hard to sit with. Drinking is romanticized and tied to so many activities. It's common to think that you can't have fun or relax without booze. Need to unwind after a long day at work? Crack open a beer! Having trouble balancing the demands of work and parenthood? Have a glass of rosé! And the more you drink, the more this becomes true. Over time, alcohol negatively impacts dopamine production, making it increasingly more challenging to feel good from everyday sources of pleasure like a sunset, cat videos, or a hilarious meme sent by your best friend.

I gave up alcohol during the COVID-19 pandemic. None of my friends or family members would have ever said I was a "problem" drinker or an alcoholic. I never experienced any significant consequences from alcohol, at least none that were observable to the outside world, but alcohol began to negatively impact my mental health. In the thick of the pandemic, like many people, I was busier than ever with work. At the same time, I had no reliable childcare. I was either working or taking care of my kids. There was no end in sight, nor was there any room to do the things that brought me calm or joy, like working out, seeing friends, or going out to a restaurant. Those were some dark times. I felt stuck and couldn't see a way out. Like many, alcohol became a too-frequent treat and a negative way of coping during those dark days. After a while, I got a message from the universe. I don't know how to describe it except to say that I got an intuitive sense that I could achieve my goals if I agreed to give up alcohol. So I did. What else was I going to do? When the universe sends a message, I listen.

After a while of not boozing, a miraculous thing started to happen. I felt like a badass. I could have fun and dance at parties stone-cold sober. Now, whenever I meet someone new, our connection isn't based on the false sense of intimacy that a couple of glasses of wine brings. And I am present for it all—the good, the frustrating, the sad, and the beautiful. Giving up alcohol at this particular point in my life was the right call for me personally. However, I would never judge someone else for drinking. Everyone must decide for themselves what they want their relationship with alcohol to look like. It's a very personal choice; my goal is to provide you with the information to make an informed one. The last thing you need is your alcohol use to unravel all the good work you do to stay mentally well.

If you are working hard to manage your mental health but still feel stressed, you may want to reevaluate your drinking habits. The question to ask yourself is not "Am I an alcoholic?" but "Is my current alcohol use serving me?"[10] Is alcohol adding to your life or detracting from it? If you are unsure, consider taking a short break from using alcohol and seeing how you feel. That information can inform your next steps in the future. Can you drink alcohol without it dulling your sparkle?[11] I hope you can be intentional about drinking to feel your best, mentally and physically.

Sobriety is also an empowering move. When you're intoxicated, you're more likely to engage in actions that are not aligned with your values and ethics. You give away your creativity, intelligence, health, clear-headedness, and financial and physical power. I'm never giving that power away again. Just think about what you could accomplish if you stopped drinking or became more mindful about your alcohol use.

Action Items

1. As you go about your week, notice when your nervous system is activated—in other words, when you feel yourself ramping up or shutting down. Check in with yourself and ask yourself what you need at that moment. Pick one nervous system hack to implement in that moment.

2. Before you go to bed each night, write down three things for which you are thankful. Remember that these can be simple or profound.

3. If you have been questioning your relationship with alcohol or thinking about cutting back, see what it's like to take a week-long (or even month-long!) hiatus from booze. After the end of the week (or month), see what changes you notice in your mood, energy, and thinking, and decide where to go from there.

CHAPTER 4

MANAGING ALL THE FEELS

Between stimulus and response there is a space. In that space is our power to choose our response. In our response lies our growth and freedom.

—Unknown

Emotional Regulation: Check Yourself Before You Wreck Yourself

I have not, historically, been good with emotional regulation. I am from the Midwest. Our answer to questions about our well-being is always "I'm fine." If we get mad at someone, all we will say is "Gosh, Debbie, your Tater Tot casserole sure is delicious. Is that cream of mushroom soup and cream cheese in there?" As I navigated adulthood, I engaged in this pattern of pretending everything was okay. I thought I was so easy breezy. I could handle it all! Until I wasn't okay and I couldn't take it. Then everything would bubble up to the surface. And by bubble up to the surface, I mean lots of ugly crying and dumping my emotions onto my mom.

I remember one time I was working part time for a company. They tasked me with doing the full-time jobs of several people. At the same time, I was undergoing fertility treatments (so there was the added stress of raging hormones, uncertainty about procreating, and mounting medical expenses—hooray!). I was frustrated and overwhelmed. And angry about making part-time money for full-time work. So I kicked a trash can really hard at work one day. A guy down the hallway asked what the noise was. I lied and said the trash can fell over. I'm a grown-ass woman who responded to her emotions by kicking a trash can. I'm not proud of it, but I suppose I can feel good about the fact that I didn't kick a person instead?

Reflecting back on that time, I can see my lack of professional boundaries was partly to blame (more on that in the next chapter). I needed to reassess my workload and be honest about what I could handle. I understand now that I couldn't juggle all my projects independently and should have asked for help. I also needed to learn how to manage overwhelming emotions instead of resorting to ineffective behaviors like kicking a trash can. This reflects the basis of emotional regulation, which involves being able to control your emotions rather than living reactively.

To understand the difference between emotional regulation and emotional reactivity, suppose you are new in your career and are up for promotion soon. However, you have this really annoying coworker who often misses deadlines. You are rightly annoyed and need to do something about it. Emotional reactivity would involve screaming, "It's on the freaking calendar, you moron! How often do I have to tell you this, or can you not read?" Emotional regulation, on the other hand, would involve sending them an email that says, "I think there has been some confusion about the deadlines. Can we clarify the schedule?" Managing your emotions allows you to think before you react so that you do not jeopardize your career advancement and work relationships.

There are several goals of emotional regulation. The first goal is to be able to name and recognize what you are feeling. Although it might be easy to know when you are feeling mad, sad, or happy, it can take some practice to know when you are feeling bored, embarrassed, insecure, or indifferent. The second goal is to limit how often and intensely you feel uncomfortable emotions, which you can often accomplish by making certain lifestyle changes. This is known as decreasing your emotional vulnerability. Finally, the third goal is to reduce emotional suffering by letting go of painful emotions that keep you stuck. In this chapter, I'll review the tools you need to accomplish all of these goals.

Fact-Checking Your Feels: Common Myths about Emotions

Not everything you've been told about emotions is true, so before getting into the details of emotional regulation, let's clear up a few misconceptions. This is especially important if you feel emotions intensely, have a history of abuse or trauma, or didn't have the best models of emotional regulation growing up.

Myth #1: Showing Emotion Is a Sign of Weakness

In our society, we have been culturally conditioned to tamp down our emotions. For example, men are often given the message that they will be seen as weak if they show emotion, while women are told that they should avoid expressing anger for the sake of "being nice." There may be other reasons you hide your feelings from others as well. For example, you may hide your desire for a committed relationship because you don't want to scare off a potential partner. Or you might be so focused on achieving a particular goal that you put off feeling grief from the death of a parent.

The reality is that it takes a lot of physical and cognitive energy to hold in your emotions, which can cause significant stress on your body. In fact, when you suppress your emotions, it causes a spike in

79

cortisol levels, which increases the risk of health issues like heart disease and cancer. Suppressing your emotions also makes it hard to attune to others, which can make others perceive you as less likable. This is not to mention that you can only push down your emotions for so long before they come bubbling back up to the surface and explode.

Myth #2: Certain Emotions Are Bad

Emotions are not intrinsically good or bad. In fact, emotions are sources of valuable information that help you operate in the world. In this sense, emotions are actually adaptive. Fear helps you avoid dangerous situations. Guilt tells you when you have screwed up and need to make amends. Anger lets you know when you've been wronged or when something needs to change. Sadness is a signal that you have lost something of value, whether a person or a goal. Therefore, even though certain emotions may feel unpleasant, this does not make them "bad."

Myth #3: Everything You Feel Must Be True

As you learned in chapter 2, just because you feel something doesn't make it true. For example, if you get stood up on a date, you might feel like an unattractive loser, but this isn't reality. You just had a really shitty night. If you make a mistake at work, you might feel like an incompetent moron, but just because you made an error doesn't mean you are a terrible employee until the end of all time. You are human, and guess what? Humans make mistakes.

Therefore, it is only sometimes in your best interest to use your emotions as a guide. For example, if you feel anxious and assume this means you are in danger, you are likely to avoid taking action even though it's in your best interest to do so. There have been plenty of times when my anxiety told me to avoid something I needed to face. Like this morning, when I had to write a difficult email. My emotions told me to distract myself with other work, but I knew I would ultimately feel calmer once I sent the email.

Myth #4: There Is a "Right" Way to Feel in Every Situation

People react to different situations in unique ways. Your best friend might be really excited that Halloween is over because she loves to decorate for Christmas, when you wish it could be spooky season all year long and are bummed out that haunted houses are over until next year. Neither of you is wrong. The culture you grew up in also impacts how you express these emotions. For example, I have several clients from East Asian families, where the display of emotions, particularly negative emotions, is frowned upon. For these clients, emotional suppression is a way to promote relational harmony and interdependence in the family system.

Myth #5: Life Would Be Dull without Extreme Emotion

Your life can be just as rich and exciting without being on an emotional roller coaster. The reality is that when you experience overwhelming and extreme emotions, you're more likely to act on those emotions by engaging in impulsive, ineffective behavior. By more skillfully managing your feelings, you can avoid these negative consequences. I was once ticked off at my in-laws because I didn't feel heard. Did I express this to them calmly and directly? No, I did not. I had too many glasses of wine and sang "Danny Boy" at the top of my lungs (multiple times). I now do a much better job of assertively communicating my needs and boundaries, and my life is still interesting.

Stepping Off the Roller Coaster

You do not have to be at the mercy of your emotions—they are not hardwired reactions in your brain over which you have no control. You have more power than you think. Feeling more in control of your emotions takes practice, but it's possible with a few simple steps.[12] I wish this were part of the junior-high-school curriculum so I could have avoided that awkward "Danny Boy" incident. But there is no time like the present to get better at being in (and out of) your feelings.

Step 1: Breathe!

Yeah, you guessed it. The first step to managing dysregulated emotions is to calm down your nervous system by taking slow belly breaths. I am sure you are pretty tired of me telling you to breathe at this point. But I mention it (again) because it is such an important tool to nip negative spirals in the bud.

As the saying goes, if you want to get out of a hole, first you have to put down the shovel. In other words, you can't effectively problem solve if you are emotionally reactive. Breathing is an easy way to bring down that reactivity. If you don't slow yourself down, you might do something rash like cut your own bangs in the bathroom mirror. Or get a tattoo of what you think are the Japanese characters for "strength, courage, and peace," only to find out later that they actually mean "beef with noodles."

Step 2: Observe what you are feeling in your mind and body.

The next step is to notice what's happening in your mind and body. What thoughts, feelings, and physical sensations are occurring? For example, you might notice your heart beating faster, your stomach or head hurting, and your skin feeling hot and sweaty. Then put a name to the feeling you are experiencing and say it to yourself without judgment: "I notice I am having feelings of anxiety, and that's okay."

When you can put a name to your experience, it helps reengage your upstairs thinking brain and decrease your emotional reactivity.

Step 3: Remind yourself that these feelings and this situation are temporary.

What you feel right now may be uncomfortable, but you will not feel this way forever. Like ocean waves on the shore, feelings come and go. Therefore, managing emotions is like surfing a wave. You don't try to suppress or block the wave of emotion, nor do you intensify it or let the feeling consume you. You simply ride the wave until your emotions eventually subside, like a wave washing onto the sand.

Step 4: Get curious.

Ask yourself, what activated your emotions? Why did your buttons get pushed at this particular moment? Oftentimes, our emotional buttons get pushed when someone steps on a closely held belief or value that we have about ourselves or the world. (You'll learn about values in chapter 8.) For example, one of my clients greatly values efficiency. He gets his work done quickly and likes to save time. He would become extremely frustrated when his coworkers started going off topic or continued meetings beyond the allotted time. He would react by becoming snippy or irritable. By learning to regulate his emotions, he can now take some deep breaths when meetings go off track and calmly redirect his coworkers.

Step 5: Take action.

By this step, you have hopefully tempered some of that initial emotional reactivity. Now, you can engage in more efficient problem-solving. What would help your current situation? What is the most logical and rational course of action? If you felt emotionally overwhelmed because there are too many things on your to-do list, can you ask for help or better prioritize those tasks? Or if there is a challenging conversation you have been avoiding with a coworker, perhaps now is the time to have that talk since you have taken a moment to organize your thoughts and feelings.

I used these five steps the other day during an interaction with my four-year-old. Preschoolers are savage, y'all. This particular tiny human is the one I mentioned earlier who refused to brush her hair and was starting to look like an unkempt orphan from the musical *Annie*. We were getting ready for school, and it was time to do something with her hair (cue the scary music). Unsurprisingly, she threw an epic preschooler meltdown, yelled, and ran away from me and the hairbrush.

Fortunately for me, I had been researching emotional regulation strategies, so I took a couple of deep breaths. I realized I was feeling frustrated, annoyed, and helpless. I thought, *I'm a crappy mom because I can't even get my kid ready for school properly*, and *We can't be late again.* I then reminded myself that it was okay to feel frustrated and overwhelmed. I got curious about what might be contributing to the situation. I remembered that I am a morning person. Mornings are my jam. I was incredibly frustrated that this preschooler was disrupting my zen and starting my day off on a sour note.

I asked myself what would ultimately help the situation. I decided it was time to get this little gal to the salon, and I booked a hair appointment for that same day. My kiddo now has a super cute, short bob. She complains that she would rather have long hair like Rapunzel, but the past few mornings have been much less dramatic. Emotional regulation for the win! (At least this time. Feel free to check in again when I have teenagers.)

In the rest of this chapter, I'll present several additional strategies you can use to step off the emotional roller coaster and learn to manage all the feels. It all comes down to being proactive, increasing your mindfulness game, and practicing emotional acceptance.

PLEASE Be on Top of Your Self-Care Game

Being proactive is about reducing your vulnerability to strong emotions. It is tough to control your emotions if your self-care game is off. Let's say you stayed up all night watching *Game of Thrones* on HBO while drinking a six-pack. The following day, your boss gives you a really frustrating assignment that needs to be done by the close of business. Do you think you will react to your boss calmly, coolly, and collectedly? Yeah, I didn't think so either.

To reduce your vulnerability to emotions, try following the steps in the acronym PLEASE. You'll notice these steps look a heck of a lot like the information you learned in the self-care chapter, which is why I can't emphasize the importance of self-care enough:

- Address PhysicaL illness. See your doctor regularly, get diagnostic tests if necessary, and take any medication as prescribed.

- Eat regular and balanced meals. Make sure to take time for meals and snacks. Work toward habits that will nourish your body, like increasing your intake of fruits and vegetables, decreasing your consumption of refined sugar, and eating a balance of fat, protein, and fiber to keep your blood sugar stable.

- Avoid substances that alter your mind, such as alcohol, nicotine, caffeine, illegal drugs, and prescriptions that are not prescribed to you. Mind-altering substances often serve as a substitute for more positive coping strategies.

- Sleep enough hours each night. As we talked about before, getting the right amount of quality sleep is essential to mental health!

- Exercise, stretch, or move your body in ways you enjoy so you can reap the benefits of less anxiety, better sleep, and improved physical health.

Stop Shoulding on Yourself

Although it is common for people to judge themselves when they have certain emotions, this only makes them feel even worse. For example, if I feel down, I might tell myself, *I shouldn't be sad! I've got so many great things going on in my life.* And now I've added guilt and shame on top of the sadness. To stop this vicious cycle, I often tell my clients to name their emotions and add the phrase "and that's okay" at the end of the statement. If you are at your wit's end with your young kids, try telling yourself, *I am feeling frustrated, and that's okay.* When you stop shoulding on yourself, it gives you a chance to deal with your emotions productively.

You can also ask yourself what this emotion is trying to tell you. If this emotion could talk, what would it say? If you feel irritated, perhaps that emotion is a signal that you need a break. If you feel envious, that emotion is giving you essential insight into what might be lacking in your life. You can then ask yourself what you need instead of berating yourself for feeling a certain way.

Acceptance Is Rad

Another strategy for managing all the feels is radical acceptance. When you practice radical acceptance, you acknowledge that some situations are outside your control and accept reality without judgment. Imagine looking out the window and noticing that it's rainy, cloudy, and gray outside. In turn, you think, *This sucks. I hate the rain. I have all this stuff I want to do today!* This thought is likely to make you feel resentful and irritable, am I right? An alternative is to think, *Yeah, it's raining today* and go about your day anyway. The latter is an attitude of radical acceptance. You don't assume that there is anything personal about the rain. It's not like the rain is out to get you. The rain just is.

I've been practicing radical acceptance lately because all sorts of illnesses have made the rounds in my kids' preschool and elementary school. My kids have been under the weather frequently this fall and winter. (I'm kicking myself for not buying that portable upholstery cleaner on Black Friday this year. That would have come in handy for all the barfing happening around my house.) I am a planner by nature, but recently, I've had to throw out any expectations for my day or week due to my kids getting sick. Practicing radical acceptance has helped me avoid wasting mental energy wondering why this is happening and feeling cheated out of my plans.

Radical acceptance doesn't mean you have to be happy about the situation. I don't love the fact that my kids are out of school and that I'm cleaning up barf. But radical acceptance does mean that I accept the reality of this less-than-ideal situation instead of fighting against it. I can't change the fact that one of my kids puked three times between the hours of midnight and 2:00 a.m. And refusing to accept this reality won't change the fact that it happened. It will only turn my pain into suffering.

To practice radical acceptance, you'll want to begin by mindfully observing your thoughts whenever you find yourself in a difficult or uncomfortable situation that is out of your control. Notice whenever you are having thoughts like these:

- I can't do this.

- Why is this happening to me?

- Life isn't fair.

- I can't handle this right now.

These sorts of thoughts reflect a lack of acceptance, which brings about feelings of anger, frustration, and hopelessness. This can lead to negative coping behaviors, such as binge drinking, impulse shopping, and numbing out on your phone. Radical acceptance, on the other hand, involves shifting your thoughts to ones like these:

- It is what it is.

- I will focus on what is in my control.

- I can't change the situation, but I can change my perspective.

- I accept that some things are out of my control.

- I can handle challenging situations.

Practicing radical acceptance increases the likelihood that you will respond to a challenging situation with logic and reason. This way of thinking embodies growth, hopefulness, and resilience. It also makes it easier to experience both joy and pain at the same time. You may feel disappointed that your soccer game is canceled when the forecast calls for rain, but that means you might get a chill day watching Netflix. Pretty rad.

HALT

HALT is an acronym often used in addiction treatment to prevent relapse, but it can benefit anyone looking to manage their emotions. The literal definition of the word *halt* is "to stop and pause." I want you to do the same when you feel a strong emotion and then use HALT to investigate that feeling by asking if you are hungry, angry, lonely, or tired/thirsty.

Hungry

If anxiety is ramping up, or you feel down and low in energy, ask yourself when you last had something to eat. Did you have breakfast today? Do you need to eat lunch? No shame in needing a snack. Maybe we could fix Congress if we made them all sit down at 3:00 p.m. and have some peanut butter and crackers. You will also want to put some thought into what you are eating. Protein and fiber will keep your blood sugar steady, keeping your mood more stable. A bag of gummy bears isn't going to help. Trust me, I've tried.

Angry

Did someone tick you off? Are you feeling resentful or taken advantage of? If so, be curious about that feeling. Do you need to speak up and say something? Or do you need to do some jumping jacks or walk around the block to discharge that tension? Pay close attention to what anger and resentment are trying to tell you. It usually means that something's got to give, and a better boundary may be necessary.

Lonely

Authentic and meaningful human connection is an effective antidote to complicated feelings. It can be incredibly healing to know that you are not alone. If you are feeling overwhelmed, find a way to connect with someone, even in a small way. Text a friend to say that you are thinking of them, send someone a postcard, thank or tip someone working in retail, or give a compliment to a stranger. Many more people are working from home these days, so it can take more effort to find social outlets. If you feel isolated, consider finding a class or activity to incorporate social connection into your week.

Thirsty or Tired

Regulating your emotions will be much more challenging if you are tired or dehydrated. If you are feeling off, get yourself a glass of water. Take a 5- or 10-minute nap, even if that means closing your eyes for a few minutes in your car. I promise that a nap will deliver a better payoff than scrolling on your phone for the same amount of time.

Roll with the Changing Seasons

There's a reason why it feels like everyone popped a Molly when the first warm and sunny day of spring rolls around. As humans, we are biologically wired to be outdoors when the sun is shining and to tuck ourselves into bed when the sun sets. This is what supports our circadian rhythm—that internal clock that regulates various biological and physiological processes.

It should thus come as no surprise that the change in seasons can significantly impact your mood. The changing seasons can kick you right in the feels. When the weather gets colder and the days get shorter, it means there is less sunlight to go around, and your brain produces less serotonin, which is a feel-good hormone. The change in seasons can also impact your melatonin levels, which affects mood and sleep patterns. This can cause you to have less energy, want more sleep, feel more irritable, and have less motivation for social and pleasurable activities. You are not alone if you feel the urge during the fall and winter to cocoon yourself in a blanket and watch Ree Drummond make casseroles on episodes of *The Pioneer Woman*.

If the change of seasons greatly impacts your day-to-day functioning, consider spending more time outside during the winter months or trying light therapy (which involves the use of a special light box to increase light exposure). You might also touch base with your doctor or a health care professional to see if vitamin D supplements or medication is right for you.

Fa La La La La ... Fuck the Holidays

When I was a freshman in high school, my dad died on Christmas day after being sick with cancer for a long time. Please note that I did not say he "lost his battle with cancer." Having an illness is not like playing in a football game or fighting in a war. There is no winning or losing. If someone dies from a disease, it wasn't because they didn't try hard enough or lacked the will to live. My dad also isn't a cancer "victim." It's not like cancer pulled a knife on him in a back alley and tried to steal his wallet. The hard truth is that some people get better and others don't. Thank you for coming to my TED Talk.

Unsurprisingly, I am not always a bundle of holiday cheer. I just texted my brother that I am sick of Christmas and want to make myself feel better by buying expensive shoes. He replied that I should buy two pairs, which is why I love my brother.

I used to get a sinking feeling in my stomach and a clenched jaw when I saw the first holiday commercial of the year, which was usually right after Halloween. I'd be eating leftover Swedish Fish and then see that holiday luxury car commercial. The one where some wealthy dingus in a Fair Isle sweater surprises their partner with a fancy car adorned with a giant bow. Seriously, who makes a significant financial purchase like that without telling their spouse? And where do they get those gigantic bows? I also used to get all ragey at certain Christmas songs on the radio, particularly the one referring to the "hap-happiest season of all!" Sure, it's the happiest season of all. Until someone dies. (If you have a dark sense of humor, let's hang out sometime!)

Nowadays, I have made peace with the holiday season (because I like presents, cookies, and shiny stuff). Still, I recognize that I am not alone in my complex feelings toward the holidays. I doubt that many of us have festivities that resemble the commercials we see on television—you know, those with the cheery family typically consisting of a White, wealthy, heterosexual couple with two kids and a set of healthy and supportive grandparents in the background. And, naturally, that family wears matching pajamas next to a perfectly decorated Christmas tree, a Honey Baked Ham, and a giant stack of beautifully wrapped presents.

There's this expectation that we should be these vessels of gratitude, joy, and peace during the holidays, but often we feel anything but that. Most of us have to manage financial concerns, addiction, family conflict, grief, caregiving, and competing demands amid the holiday season. You show up to Thanksgiving dinner knowing that your gram will ask you when she's getting grandkids. Meanwhile, you are on round two of IVF treatment for infertility. You'd like to bring your same-sex partner to meet your extended family, but your uncle will go on a political rant or start quoting his fire-and-brimstone pastor once he is three beers in. Or, at a minimum, you'd like your Hanukkah holiday party to look like Martha Stewart was in charge, but you are on a tight budget and lack Martha's extensive staff of chefs and decorators.

If you don't feel festive or joyous during the holiday season, there is nothing wrong with you. The holidays can be stressful, complicated, and messy. Accept the range of emotions you might feel, up your self-care during this time, and practice healthy boundaries (more on that in the next chapter). I don't know who needs to hear this, but keeping the holidays simple is perfectly okay. If certain traditions have lost their luster for you, skip or adapt those activities. No one will care if you don't send out greeting cards. (And if they do care, that's their problem, not yours!) If gift giving is out of your budget this year, have a frank conversation with your loved ones about what you can and can't afford. Do the best you can to manage the holiday season. And remember that no one's life looks like a perfectly staged holiday commercial. I bet even the Virgin Mary got ticked off at the three wise men on the first Christmas for bringing her frankincense, gold, and myrrh instead of coffee, diapers, and wipes.

Create a Coping Card or Kit

It's tough to figure out what to do when your emotions get overwhelming. When that downstairs emotional brain of yours takes control, remember that your upstairs thinking brain goes offline, making it difficult to think rationally about your best choice of action. In these moments, it can be helpful to have a prepared list of coping strategies that can help you feel better. Making this list in advance will allow you to be ready when the going gets tough.

Some of my clients like to create a coping card that they can laminate and fit in their wallet, while others prefer to keep a list on their phone. Other clients find it helpful to create a physical coping kit by filling a decorative box with stress-reducing ideas. Here are a few things you can consider putting in your coping tool kit:

- Inspirational quotes or affirmations

- Mindful breathing exercises

- Links to meditation apps

- Playlists to suit different moods

- Stress balls, fidget toys, modeling clay, slime, or bubble wrap to pop

- A list of your favorite movies or shows

- Names of people you can call, text, or write for support

- A list of nervous system hacks (e.g., doing 25 jumping jacks, splashing cold water on your face)

- Fun or beautiful stationery and stamps

- Coloring books for adults, collage materials, and art supplies

- Scented candles or essential oils associated with stress relief (e.g., lavender, ylang-ylang, lemon, rosemary)

- Tea, candy, or snacks

- A favorite book

- Funny cartoons or memes

- Numbers for crisis support lines

You can also create a coping tool kit for a friend who is having a hard time. Next year for the holidays, I am making a coping basket for everyone on my list. I'll be like Oprah passing out cars. You get a coping skill! And you get a coping skill! Everybody gets coping skills!

When Things Get Really Dark

There can be times in your life when you feel so overwhelmed that it's hard to see a way out. I'm here to tell you that many people have passive thoughts about not wanting to be around anymore, wishing they were dead, or not wanting to wake up in the morning. You are not alone if you have those thoughts, nor are you "crazy" or "weird." People may have thoughts about ending their life if they are experiencing:

- Isolation and hopelessness

- Severe mental illness

- Financial hardship

- Addiction

- The end of a significant relationship

- A chronic or terminal illness

- A traumatic brain injury

- Bullying, abuse, or violence

- Feelings of shame

There is a significant difference between passive and active suicidal ideation. Passive suicidality is about wanting your pain to end, thinking about what it would be like to not be here anymore, or desiring to escape from your problems. When you have passive suicidal ideation, you may have thoughts of ending your life (*I wish I could go to sleep and not wake up*, *My family would be better off without me*, or *I want it all to stop*) but no actual plans to carry it out. In contrast, active suicidal ideation involves thinking about specific ways in which to end your life. This is more serious than passive suicidal ideation because it involves the intent to die and a plan to carry it out. Someone with active suicidal ideation might gather the means to end their life, detach from others and their activities, or give away personal items.

While passive suicidal ideation does not usually represent an immediate risk of death, it should still be taken seriously since it can progress into active suicidality. It can also lead people to behave recklessly and engage in actions that put them in harm's way (e.g., not wearing their seatbelt, driving while under the influence). They may not be actively trying to end their lives, but they are still engaging in behaviors that could have this end result. Therefore, it's critical to evaluate your risk of self-harm if you have passive suicidal thoughts. If you wish life would end but have no specific plan to harm yourself, this is an excellent time to reach out to a trusted friend or family member. Get their support in brainstorming and identifying your next steps for mental health treatment. If something changed in your life, would you feel better or different? That question can give you essential information on what to focus on next. (More information on how to go about seeking mental health services is discussed in chapter 9.)

Take immediate steps to stay safe if you are thinking about how or when you might end your life and have access to lethal means (e.g., you have pills or a firearm in your house). Reach out to someone you trust in your community, dial 988 to reach the National Suicide and Crisis Lifeline, or go to a behavioral health urgent care center or emergency room. What you feel right now is intense and real, but help is available. You are worth it, and healing is possible. Give yourself that chance.

Action Items

1. Think about a recent time when you felt intense emotions. Reflect on what might have contributed to the situation. Were you hungry, tired, or thirsty? Did you spend any time outside that day? Were any of your beliefs or values violated?

2. Identify someone who brings up feelings of envy in you. What does that person have that you would like to have in your own life? How can you use those feelings to take action?

3. If you currently feel anxious or down, how can you reduce those feelings by just 5 percent? Even if many things are out of your control, what remains in your control?

4. How can you practice radical acceptance in your life in big and small ways? What are some things that you struggle to accept?

CHAPTER 5

HEALTHY BOUNDARIES ARE BADASS

 Compassionate people ask for what they need. They say no when they need to, and when they say yes, they mean it. They're compassionate because their boundaries keep them out of resentment.

—Brené Brown

What Are Boundaries?

Boundaries are such a beautiful thing. I never thought much about boundaries until I became a parent, and everything became limited. I had limited time, energy, and patience. Boundaries became a lifeline for protecting my peace. As Robin Arzón, a popular fitness instructor, often says, "Boundaries are sexy." I couldn't agree more.

I define boundaries as the limits you set to protect your mental, emotional, and physical well-being. The concept of boundaries is similar to having a fence around your yard. Boundaries serve as your personal property line, letting other people know the limits of what you are (and are not) comfortable with. Setting boundaries is not about punishing or harming someone else. It is about knowing what you need in order to be your best self, maintain relationships, and bring more contentment to your life. Boundaries help protect against burnout and prevent you from feeling used or angry. They help you create physical, emotional, and mental safety.

Boundaries can fall into one of three categories: porous, rigid, or healthy. Here, I'll discuss each type of boundary in greater detail and then discuss how you can set better boundaries and communicate more effectively regarding your wants and needs.

Porous Boundaries

When someone does not set limits, their boundaries can be considered porous or weak. This is akin to having no fence in your yard: Anyone can come in, eat your nachos, put their feet on your lovely lawn furniture, and throw trash around. Not good. Making a deluxe plate of nachos takes effort, and I am not sharing them with just anyone.

You may struggle with porous boundaries if you:

- Have a hard time saying no to others

- Need to go along with the group or comply

- Often feel taken advantage of or feel like a victim

- Overshare personal information

- Become overly involved with the problems of others

- Seek the opinions of others before making decisions

- Have drama-filled relationships

- Keep the peace at a cost to your personal well-being

- Feel anxious and guilty a lot

- Need to be liked by everyone

- Tend to be passive-aggressive instead of directly communicating what you need or want

- Tolerate disrespect or abuse

That woman at a recent networking happy hour you just met who told you about her colonoscopy and gave a play-by-play of her last marriage counseling session? Yeah, those would be porous boundaries.

Rigid Boundaries

When someone has rigid boundaries, they tend to keep people at a distance to protect themselves from getting hurt. This is like having a giant brick wall around your yard that is 10 feet high and topped with barbed wire. Nobody can get in (and nobody would want to, for that matter, because you would be that weirdo neighbor who lives in an impenetrable fortress!).

You may have rigid boundaries if you:

- Have a hard time asking for help
- Are reluctant to rely on other people
- Guard your personal information closely
- Are unwilling to try things outside your comfort zone
- Fear abandonment and rejection
- Tend to keep people at an arm's distance
- Avoid close relationships and intimacy

The coworker you've sat next to at work for three years and whom you know precisely nothing about except that he eats a turkey sandwich for lunch every day? He may have rigid boundaries.

Healthy Boundaries

Finally, a person with healthy boundaries knows how to set limits that prioritize their well-being and can adapt these limits to individual circumstances. You can think of healthy boundaries as having a nice picket fence around your yard with a gate you can open and close at your convenience. You can easily wave to the UPS driver across the street and let in friends who pass by, but stray dogs and drunk college students stay out. You keep the good in (your nachos) and the bad out (trash-throwing neighbors).

You likely have healthy boundaries if you:

- Say no to requests that do not align with your priorities or personal values

- Have no tolerance for abuse and disrespect

- Insist on being treated with dignity

- Carefully protect your time, energy, and resources

- Avoid relying on input from others to make critical decisions

- Are okay with not always being liked

- Have the ability to identify and express your emotions

- Feel a sense of ownership over your own life and goals

- Are confident in what you believe, like, and value

Your sister who always tells you how long she can talk on the phone before going to bed so she can get enough rest for tomorrow? Girl's got some good boundaries.

Figuring Out Your Fuck Budget and the Art of Saying No

You only have so many fucks to give in life, am I right? Having healthy boundaries allows you to spend your fucks wisely. That's why it is essential to figure out your fuck budget. In her insightful TED Talk, "The Magic of Not Giving a Fuck," bestselling author Sarah Knight explained that your "fucks" are your time, energy, and money.[13] Your fucks are what you care about. Having a fuck budget means that you spend your fucks on the things that are meaningful to you. Once you have figured out your fuck budget, you can more easily say no to the things you don't care about and make space for the things that bring you meaning.

For example, I give a fuck about my family and friends, cooking, reading, writing, and getting a lot of sleep. I don't give a fuck about football, hanging out in noisy bars, or fad diets. Therefore, I am not going to spend any of my hard-earned money buying tickets to football games. I am not going to accept any invitations that involve staying up late in dive bars (no way am I sacrificing my precious sleep). I will, however, say yes to hanging out with friends in coffee shops and buying more kitchen gadgets and books than necessary.

The beautiful thing about saying no is that you don't have to give a reason! Although there can be pressure to justify your reasoning, you don't need to defend your choice. To clarify, this does not mean that you have a free pass to be a dick. You can be polite and kind when turning down requests for your time, energy, and money. For example, let's say a colleague invites me to a networking happy hour, and I don't want to go. I have plans to go home and reorganize my pantry. (We all have different ideas of fun, okay?) All I need to say to my colleague is "Thank you so much for the invitation, but I can't make it. I hope you have a great time!" That, my friends, is the power of the word *no*.

Here are a few different ways to say no that are handy to have in your back pocket:

- "That sounds really fun, but I have other plans."

- "That's not in my budget this month, but thank you for thinking of me."

- "I wish I could help you, but I have other commitments."

- "I'm not able to meet then, but I would love to see you another time."

- "This isn't a good time for me to talk."

- "No, thank you."

- "I can't right now, but I will let you know if anything changes."

- "I am thrilled that you want me in your wedding party / at your birthday in Bali / on your graduation trip to Vegas, but my budget doesn't allow me to participate in all the planned festivities. Can we talk about other ways I can support you on your big day?"

- "If I take on that task, I will not have time to complete my other project. Which would you like to prioritize?"

How to Know When You Need a Boundary

When figuring out when you need a boundary in your life, emotions are an essential source of information. If you notice that you are feeling annoyed, angry, used, or exhausted, that's a sign that something has got to give. This is especially important if you tend to be a compassionate, giving person or if you have people-pleasing tendencies. I want you to be generous with others because you genuinely want to, not out of obligation or fear of letting others down.

One of my clients, Rachel, was a successful consultant at a large company. She was new in her career but had recently received several promotions. She now managed other people and wanted to be a good leader, so she avoided giving her employees work that she wouldn't do herself. She also sought to shield her team from stress and working overtime. I appreciated that Rachel was concerned about being a good supervisor, but it was at a great cost. She was having a difficult time saying no to requests and was unable to delegate tasks to her team. She gave her time and energy too freely to anyone who asked. As a result, Rachel always felt tired, no matter how much rest she got over the weekend. She also started to get the "Sunday scaries"—that feeling of dread that creeps in before the start of the work week. She also became more irritable and resentful when employees needed her attention.

During our sessions, Rachel learned that she needed to be more protective of her time and energy. She used "away" messages more often to let her colleagues know when she was working on a project that needed her complete focus. She also started delegating tasks to her team members and pausing before automatically saying yes to requests and meetings. As a result, Rachel felt less overwhelmed. She began to feel excited again about mentoring the younger members of her team. And she no longer got that anxious feeling in her stomach on Sunday nights.

Reasons Why You Might Have a Hard Time Setting Boundaries

You're Afraid of Upsetting Others

Let's say you decide the time has come to set limits in your life. You identify the boundary needed, perhaps deciding that you will no longer cook Thanksgiving dinner for 30 people. Even though you are the best cook in your family, you have work obligations and are eight months pregnant this year. Being the head chef is not gonna work. So you clearly communicate that boundary to your family: "Hey, family, I can no longer cook Thanksgiving dinner this year. Let's talk about alternative plans or have a potluck." In return, your family graciously says, "We totally understand. Thank you for having the strength to speak up." That might be the outcome if your family takes after the Brady Bunch. But if you don't happen to be living in an idealistic '70s sitcom, your grandmother will likely clutch her pearls, wail about family traditions falling apart, and ask why you don't love her anymore.

This is why setting boundaries is easier said than done. One of the main reasons that setting boundaries can be problematic is that you risk upsetting other people. Your friends and family can have a tough time when you start interacting with them differently and setting limits. You're changing the rules of the game, which can bring up feelings of guilt for you, and anger or frustration for others. It can feel like you are being selfish in putting yourself first.

Remember my inner critic, Nelson? Before I understood the concept of boundaries, Nelson would often surface when I tried to set limits in my own life. Conversations with Nelson often looked like this:

LIZ: I think I am going to decline this invitation. I really need to catch up on sleep. I need some alone time.

NELSON: If you don't go to that birthday party, your friend will be mad. She'll stop inviting you to things. You'll end up a social pariah!

LIZ: That seems a little extreme. But maybe I should go even though I don't want to . . .

NELSON: It's her birthday! You have to go to birthday parties.

LIZ: I can still send her a card and text her happy birthday.

NELSON: It's not the same. You need to go!

LIZ: But I am not even that close with her. And it's at a super noisy, overcrowded bar. In other words, an introvert's seventh circle of hell.

NELSON: Yeah, but you can't let anyone down. Ever.

(Cut to me going to that birthday party, spending money I couldn't afford to buy drinks for the birthday girl, and feeling tired and resentful the next day because I didn't get my alone time.)

Setting boundaries might end up hurting someone else's feelings, but that doesn't mean you did anything wrong. You are not responsible for managing the emotional state of another person. Still, you can be compassionate when setting limits with others. You can choose your words carefully and start with minor changes.

One client of mine, Anthony, came from a big Greek family who expected him to attend every family gathering. When Anthony was younger, attending every family event was possible because most of his extended family lived in the same community. But over time, it became increasingly difficult to abide by the expectation that he be at every family party. The younger generation grew older, started creating their own families, and moved across the country. Driving hours through congested traffic several times a month became increasingly stressful. Anthony realized that he had started to resent attending these family parties rather than being genuinely excited to catch up with everyone. In turn, he started turning down family events that were too overwhelming and stressful to fit in his schedule.

Anthony knew this decision would make his mom disappointed and hurt. (And it did. She claimed that he "didn't care about his family.") But Anthony realized that his mom's reaction was out of his control. He couldn't keep the peace with his mom at the cost of his own mental well-being. While he cared about his family deeply and prioritized seeing them regularly, he valued having the weekends to decompress from his busy job. He also wanted to devote time to his relationship with his new girlfriend. Therefore, Anthony stayed firm in his decision and often felt like a broken record in discussions with his mom. He repeatedly told her that he valued his family and understood her disappointment. Still, he would not be able to attend every event. Anthony's mom never became happy with his decision, but he began to feel less stressed and more in control of his personal time.

Having Hard Conversations Is Uncomfortable

A lot of the stress I experienced when I was younger came from a fear of having hard conversations. I was afraid of letting someone down, being seen as anything other than "nice," or having others perceive me as incompetent or naive. But now I can see that the stress of not having those conversations far outweighed the temporary discomfort of speaking up.

My clients also struggle with having hard conversations. When my client Mackenzie got engaged, she didn't want a flashy bridal shower. She is an introvert and didn't feel the need for any additional household items. She said, "I already have my trusty toaster and blender, thank you very much." Mackenzie tried in her refined southern way to let her future mother-in-law know that she didn't need another party and that she would rather her in-laws use those funds for the wedding. Or even better, use those funds to save puppies, fight climate change, or help disadvantaged kids. But Mackenzie's mother-in-law's uncompromising New York attitude didn't pick up on her subtleties and she insisted on hosting a massive bridal shower. Mackenzie knew this party was important to her, so she went along with the festivities. She kept the peace at a cost to her own well-being.

Mackenzie's mother-in-law ended up having a massive luncheon at a flashy restaurant where Mackenzie had to be the center of attention for hours as she opened gifts. During the luncheon, Mackenzie's mother-in-law also strung up a clothesline behind her and read a poem she had written (or found somewhere in the deep, dark wedding-blog bowels of the internet). This poem referenced the lingerie Mackenzie would wear throughout her marriage and paid homage to her sex life with her future husband. With each stanza, her mother-in-law strung up a piece of risqué underwear and lingerie—in front of the entire restaurant and all of Mackenzie's future relatives. Mackenzie was mortified. As Mackenzie explained it to me, "I was in introvert hell."

Brené Brown says that "clear is kind. Unclear is unkind."[14] In our attempts to avoid discomfort, we often avoid being honest and direct with others. But that can lead to more problems down the line. If Mackenzie had dared to be firm about her preference to not have a bridal shower, she could have avoided the distress of being at the center of a big event. She would also have bypassed the resulting resentment and frustration toward her future mother-in-law. Nowadays, Mackenzie can reflect on the bridal-shower-turned-surprise-lingerie-party as an entertaining story. But she has since learned that she can have hard conversations if it means protecting her emotional peace. Mackenzie would tell her younger self that she is strong enough to stand her ground.

Like Mackenzie, it is important to realize that you can be direct and assert your boundary even when it feels uncomfortable. And often, you must be a broken record and restate your boundary many times before the other person realizes you are serious. Engaging in hard conversations might feel uncomfortable in the short term, but in the long run, it protects against ill will and passive-aggressive behavior. By showing up, checking your ego, and tolerating the discomfort of tough conversations, you can solve problems while maintaining respect for yourself and the other person.

You're a People Pleaser

It can also be hard to set boundaries if you are a people pleaser. People pleasers tend to fall into the porous boundary category. They seek to make others happy, often to the detriment of their own emotional well-being. They avoid conflict at all costs and will go to great lengths to prevent anyone from being mad at them. People pleasers often feel like their time isn't their own because they say yes to so many requests out of obligation, leaving less time and energy for their own priorities.

There are many reasons why individuals engage in people-pleasing behaviors. Sometimes they derive a sense of self-worth from helping others. Sometimes they feel the need for everyone to like them. Sometimes they have internalized the message that being kind and generous means always complying with others. In fact, some people pleasers grew up in chaotic or abusive families where complacency was necessary for survival. They may have had no choice but to be compliant as a child to minimize the impact of abuse or to coexist alongside a parent struggling with addiction or other challenges.

If you are a people pleaser, you might find yourself saying sorry a lot and needing to apologize for simply being a human and taking up space. When I was taking acting classes at the DC Improv, one of my fellow group members, Victor, noticed that I was apologizing way too often. I was subconsciously saying sorry just for having thoughts and opinions. He started telling me, "Stick your sorries in a sack, Liz!" I then realized I didn't have to apologize for being part of the conversation. I now only say sorry when I am genuinely regretful instead of apologizing out of nervousness. So to all of you out there apologizing for everything, stick your sorries in a sack!

And in case you need to hear this, here are a few other things you *don't* have to feel sorry about:

- Feeling confident in yourself, your expertise, and your own abilities

- Leaving a situation when you feel unsafe or uncomfortable

- Being a certain body size or looking a certain way

- Holding others accountable for their actions

- Feeling your emotions

- Taking up space in the world

- Having healthy boundaries or saying no

- Taking time for yourself to rest or recharge

- Standing up for what you believe in

- Following your dreams

You Struggle with Codependency

That scene in *Jerry Maguire* where Tom Cruise's character passionately declares "You complete me" always gave me the ick. I wanted to shout at his character, "No, dude, you are already complete! You don't need another person to complete you!" Like many others in rom-coms, that line is classic codependent behavior.

Codependency occurs when your worth and self-esteem become tied to another person. In codependent relationships, your mood, well-being, and ability to make decisions all revolve around someone else. The needs of the other person or relationship become more important than your own, making it difficult to set boundaries. Codependency often sounds like "I can't live without you" or "You are my entire world." You might catch yourself:

- Feeling like you have to get permission from the other person before making any decisions or plans

- Wanting to spend all your time with this person because being apart is uncomfortable

- Valuing the other person's opinions above your own

- Deriving a sense of purpose from the relationship and nothing else

- Being unsure of who you are outside the relationship

- Taking in the emotions of other people

- Giving out of obligation or at the expense of your own well-being

- Feeling responsible for the other person's moods and needing to fix their problems

Not surprisingly, people pleasers are at risk of codependency, whether it's with a parent, partner, or roommate. For example, my client David is an outgoing guy who greatly values the relationships in his life. During the early days of the pandemic, he was grateful that he and his roommate, Josh, were such good friends. He looked at Josh as his best friend and was thankful they could quarantine and work from home together fairly smoothly. But when the world started to open up again, David found that his life was often entangled with his roommate's. He became disappointed when Josh hung out with other friends, worried when Josh started traveling again for work, and even had difficulty making decisions, like which sports league to sign up for, without Josh's input. During our sessions, David identified that his dynamic with Josh had become codependent, and he began taking steps to maintain his friendship while developing his own identity and interests. Over time, David became more interdependent and felt less emotionally reliant on Josh for support.

Interdependence is characterized by having a distinct identity that is separate from your partner or other people. You have your own thoughts, feelings, and beliefs. You enjoy spending time together but also feel comfortable engaging in activities separately. There are healthy boundaries, clear communication, and mutual respect. In contrast to a codependent relationship, in which you and your partner are a single unit, in an interdependent relationship, you and your partner are two players on the same team.

One way to develop more interdependence is to nurture your own friendships and interests. If you love a certain Netflix series but your partner can't stand it, that's okay! Schedule some solo TV time or host a watch party with your fellow *Great British Baking Show* aficionados. Talk with your partner or bestie to make sure you have a balance of togetherness and independence.

The Basics of Assertive and Healthy Communication

I can't talk about boundaries without also talking about communication. Once you know a limit is needed, you must communicate and uphold that boundary. That is, you must be assertive. Although the word *assertive* often gets thrown around and misconstrued as having a negative connotation, assertiveness is the backbone of healthy communication. It's about recognizing that your wants and needs are just as valid as the wants and needs of others. It's about standing up for yourself in a respectful, yet firm, way to get those wants and needs met.

This is in contrast to passive communication (in which you fail to stand up for yourself), aggressive communication (in which you are overbearing or hostile), and passive-aggressive communication (in which you appear passive on the surface but act out your hostility in indirect ways).

You can sum up the difference between the four communication styles with this list:

- **Passive:** My needs don't matter. Your needs do matter. (I lose, you win.)

- **Aggressive:** My needs matter. Your needs don't matter. (You lose, I win.)

- **Passive-aggressive:** I'm hurt, or my needs aren't being met, but I am not open about my emotions and feelings. I indirectly communicate my displeasure. (I lose, you lose.)

- **Assertive:** My needs matter, and your needs matter too. We compromise. There's an understanding that both parties' feelings are valid. (I win, you win.)

For example, let's say that your roommate often brews the last of your artisanal organic coffee beans without asking, leaving you stranded without your much-needed caffeine jolt. A passive response would be to do nothing at all and just drink the shitty office coffee, an aggressive response would be to get into a shouting match and hide your coffee stash, a passive-aggressive response would be to eat your roommate's expensive snacks without asking, and an assertive response would be to have a firm, but respectful, conversation about your preferences regarding how groceries are shared.

In order to develop assertive communication, you want to describe the problem using "I" statements as much as possible. An "I" statement focuses on *your* concerns and feelings about the situation, as opposed to blaming the other person for how you feel. You want to prevent the other person from immediately going on the defensive and shutting down. Describe the impact the other person's behavior has on you. Then state what you would like to be different in the future.

One of my clients, Luisa, came from a family entrenched in diet culture. Luisa shared memories of her and her mom counting calories and keeping food diaries when she was in high school. Luisa's mother would still comment on Luisa's body and weight when Luisa would travel home to visit her family. In our sessions, Luisa and I worked toward her becoming more accepting of her body. She realized that the comments from her mother were not helping and could trigger deep-seated insecurities. She decided that her appearance and body were no longer acceptable topics of conversation. She also would not accept any comments about what and how much she was eating.

When Luisa traveled home last Thanksgiving, her mom, not unexpectedly, said, "It looks like you've gained some weight. Maybe we should skip breakfast and get in some extra workouts." Luisa was prepared with a response this time. She explained that she appreciated her mom's concern, but she no longer wanted to discuss her weight or body size: "I know you are trying to be helpful, but comments about my body make me feel insecure. I've been working hard lately to feel comfortable in my skin. From now on, please do not comment on the shape or size of my body." Then Luisa brought up their favorite reality show, *Million Dollar Listing New York*, to steer the conversation in a new direction and focus the discussion on outrageously priced real estate. Luisa's mother still slipped into her old behavior patterns at times, but Luisa had become comfortable saying, "I'm not going to discuss my weight" or "Let's talk about something more interesting than diets." If her mom pushed the topic, Luisa explained that she would leave the room or go outside for a walk if the comments about her body didn't stop.

If you clearly communicate a boundary and the other person violates that boundary, it's up to you to decide the consequences. You can reinforce the boundary once again, but if the unwanted behavior persists, you can use that information to evaluate whether or not you want to continue being in the relationship.

Setting Boundaries around Technology and Social Media

Online communities can be a great way to combat isolation. However, not every online space is emotionally and mentally safe. Remember that social media and other smartphone apps are designed to keep you scrolling and addicted. The engineers who create these apps know that their products need to generate a profit to secure money from investors. To do that, they specifically engineer the apps to draw you in so that you spend a great deal of time on them. Even the most well-intentioned person has likely gone on TikTok or Instagram for "just a few minutes" and found themselves coming up for air an hour and a half later, wondering where the hell that time went. The other day, I spent 45 minutes researching hamster and gerbil habitats before finally realizing that another pet is the last thing I need. Nothing is wrong with you or your willpower if you get sucked into your phone. They are designed to do just that.

Getting "likes" on your social media posts can also feel validating, especially when you feel lonely or isolated. Everyone wants to feel recognized and accepted by others. Receiving attention on social media feeds that desire. Unfortunately, connecting with others online is not the same as interacting with people in real-life settings. Spending too much time on social media can also lead you to compare yourself to others. You see everyone else's highlight reels and carefully curated (and retouched!) photos and wonder if your life measures up. This results in you spending less time enjoying activities in the present moment and more time thinking about whether or not you are getting the right shot or video to post on social media.

I visited an apple orchard with my kids last year. The weather was perfect. We fed the goats, drank apple cider, and bought a truckload of produce and pumpkins. I remember seeing this woman there who was dressed impeccably. She was posing by the apple trees while her friend took pictures. I guessed that she was an influencer or a wannabe influencer. I couldn't help but wonder if she was actually enjoying being at the orchard that day or was more concerned with the reactions these photos would generate. Nothing against being an influencer or sharing pictures online (I get that sometimes you want to snap a selfie on a great hair day), but I often worry that we forget to be in the moment.

Social media aside, the problem with technology is that we often use our digital devices to distract ourselves from uncomfortable feelings like stress, worry, frustration, boredom, and exhaustion. Our phones offer us entertainment if we are in an unfamiliar place, like waiting at the dentist or sitting on the bus. It's an easy way to numb out from the world, but scrolling doesn't help us find restoration or true relaxation. Another problem with technology is that since we rely on our phones for both work and personal activities, we never quite feel like we are entirely off the clock. It's easy to fall into the trap of checking work messages during personal time to stay on top of our professional tasks. Our phones also subtly pressure us to constantly be productive through fitness apps, to-do lists, incoming text messages, goal trackers, and shopping sites.

Given that technology is so addictive, setting boundaries around its use can save you from yourself. Boundaries around technology might look like:

- Charging your phone outside the bedroom at night and using an alarm clock to wake up

- Keeping your phone in another room while you are working (I have a client who locks it in her mailbox during the day!)

- Setting time limits for specific apps and features

- Using the "do not disturb" feature when you need to rest or focus

- Recognizing that you are under no obligation to return text or other messages immediately

- Unfollowing people and groups that make you feel bad about yourself

- Only attending to professional emails and activities during the workday

- Hiding or deleting apps from your home screen

- Using your phone with intention—find inspiration from Pinterest and translate it to real life (e.g., instead of just "liking" a recipe for teriyaki chicken bowls, actually make it)

- Being kind and courteous online by treating others the way you want to be treated

Finally, it's essential to set boundaries around your media consumption following traumatic events that get widespread local or national attention. You understandably want to be informed about what is happening in your community and worldwide, but you can stay informed without doom scrolling or watching hours of devastating news coverage. Find a few news outlets you trust and limit the time you spend catching up on world events. Be cautious about social media usage following a traumatic event to avoid hearing inaccurate information, being exposed to extremist views, or being blindsided by harrowing images.

Dealing with Emotional Dumpers

When it comes to setting boundaries, many conversations in my practice center around managing friends and family who engage in emotional dumping. Emotional dumping occurs when someone wants to talk to you about their problems without considering if you have the emotional capacity and time for the conversation. Oftentimes, they may go in circles as they ruminate about their problem. It's like listening to a broken record. People who emotionally dump are typically not open to solutions and are resistant to your feedback. This can lead you to feel overwhelmed, frustrated, and resentful. On the other hand, you may be emotionally dumping on others and not even realize it.

Emotional dumping is different from venting. Venting occurs when someone wants to get something off their chest, and the person doing the venting typically asks for permission before they talk about their problem. While they're open to feedback, they do not expect the other person to solve their problem or do anything about it. They also don't go in circles or monopolize the conversation—the discussion flows back and forth. Emotional dumping, on the other hand, occurs without consent and often leaves the listener feeling as if they are responsible for making the other person feel better. The listener may feel helpless to fix their friend's problem.

One of my clients, Ellie, constantly felt drained by her friendship with Tara, a friend from college. They both moved to Washington, DC, after graduation. Ellie appreciated that she and Tara had many fun memories from living in the same dorm and studying abroad together. They also both shared the experience of starting their professional lives in the nation's capital. However, the friendship began to feel one-sided. Tara would spend the entire evening complaining about her stressful job whenever she and Ellie met for happy hour or dinner. At first, Ellie was pleased to support her friend during this challenging time, but absorbing all this negativity slowly became exhausting. After all, Ellie was dealing with her own set of challenges when it came to dating, navigating her new job, and managing finances.

After Ellie and I discussed the idea of setting boundaries, she decided to start turning down Tara's requests to meet up whenever Ellie had a particularly stressful or busy week. She also decided to let Tara know how long she would be available at the beginning of phone calls or text exchanges. She would tell Tara something like "I am headed to the gym in a few, so I can only chat until 6:00 p.m." When Ellie did meet up with Tara, she became more vocal about her desire to talk about her own life. She would ask Tara questions like "Hey, when you finish telling me about your work trip, can we chat about this recent date I had?" Their conversations started to be more balanced, and Ellie began to look forward to seeing Tara again.

Similar to emotional dumping is the concept of trauma dumping. You've probably heard the term before or maybe even experienced it yourself. Trauma dumping occurs when someone shares a traumatic experience with you without considering how you will receive that challenging information. This leaves you feeling caught off guard and unable to opt out of the conversation. It is difficult to process what you have heard, and you may be unsure how to respond. This can make you feel confused, unsettled, annoyed, or drained. The following are all characteristics of trauma dumping:

- Making a sudden or unexpected disclosure about difficult content

- Disclosing traumatic experiences to someone you just met

- Discussing the same incident over and over again

- Sharing graphic details of the trauma

- Mentioning the previous trauma in casual conversation

- Posting about a challenging event online without thinking through how that information will be absorbed by others

Trauma dumping can happen between friends and family members, or it can occur with complete strangers. I was once at a bar chatting with a couple I had just met. They told me the story of having been kidnapped at gunpoint. I appreciated that they felt comfortable with me—and as a therapist, I have heard a lot throughout my career—but I was still unsure how best to respond to their disclosure compassionately, considering that we were at a dark, dingy dive bar with a "Weird Al" Yankovic lookalike singing karaoke in the background.

If you have a friend or family member who has been emotionally dumping or trauma dumping on you, there are several things you can do to protect your mental and emotional energy:

- Realize that you are not responsible for fixing your friend's problem, nor or you accountable for their happiness or mental well-being.

- Know your limits. It's perfectly okay to say, "This issue seems to have been bothering you for a while. Have you considered talking to someone with training to better support you, like a therapist or mental health professional?" If you are up to it, help your friend find mental health resources.

- Put some parameters around conversations. It's okay to tell your friend or family member that you can only talk for 15 minutes or that you aren't available to chat until later in the week. You don't have to be accessible at all times to all people.

If you realize that *you* are the person who has been doing the emotional or trauma dumping, be proud of yourself for coming to this realization. Spend some time reflecting on what might be helpful, like finding a therapist, upping your self-care game, working out your emotions in a journal, or creating art. If you are contemplating sharing vulnerable information online, think carefully about whether you are genuinely ready for everyone to know your story. If you are in a good place, being vulnerable can promote education, raise awareness, and let others know that they are not alone in their challenges. But before you post, ensure you are okay with Larry in accounting and your second-grade teacher knowing your personal information.

Above all, ask your loved ones' permission before launching into your stressors and problems. That might involve asking, "Hey, do you have a few minutes for me to talk about my relationship? Let me know if this is a good time for you."

(Now excuse me while I call my mom and apologize for all the emotional dumping I did in my 20s. Sorry, Mom!)

Action Items

1. Think about a recent time when you felt angry, irritated, or stressed. How did boundaries (or a lack of boundaries) play a role in the situation?

2. What is one healthy boundary that you can set with yourself this week?

3. Think about a time when you struggled to say no or said yes without thinking. What will you do differently in the future?

CHAPTER 6

PEOPLE NEED PEOPLE (SO FIND THE GOOD ONES)

Lots of people want to ride with you in the limo, but what you want is someone who will take the bus with you when the limo breaks down.

—Oprah Winfrey

What Healthy Relationships Look Like in Real Life

People need people. We all need to have a sense of belonging and find connection with others, but not all relationships are created equal. Some can build you up and energize you, while others can drag you down, drain you, and stunt your potential. Healthy relationships are essential to your physical and mental health, so it's important to be thoughtful about whom you'll invest your time and energy with.

It's not always easy to know what a healthy relationship looks like, particularly if you didn't grow up with models of positive communication and affection. Sometimes you may even be so charmed by someone or excited to be in a new relationship that you don't consider if this partnership is healthy. Healthy relationships involve trust, cooperation, support, honesty, safety, and accountability. Both partners respect each other. Other components of healthy relationships include:

- Enjoying each other's company
- Being able to effectively communicate with each other
- Having a sense of acceptance, trust, and belonging
- Respecting each other's boundaries
- Holding each other to realistic expectations
- Having shared values and priorities
- Resolving conflicts without resorting to name-calling, stonewalling, abuse, or violence
- Sharing hopes and dreams for the future
- Making financial decisions together
- Sharing parenting responsibilities
- Supporting each other's goals and aspirations

Of course, even in the best of relationships, major life events like buying a house, having a baby, losing a job, or changing careers can cause things to get off track. Relationships take work, and sometimes it's hard to know where to start (or where to pick up where you left off). In this chapter, you'll learn some basic tools for developing and sustaining healthy relationships, including how to meet people, identify relationship red flags, work through unhealthy attachment styles, keep the romance alive, and apologize like a pro.

Talking to Strangers

When you were a kid, you were probably told, "Don't talk to strangers!" by the grown-ups in your life. But now that you are an adult, talking to strangers is essential to expanding your sense of connection and community. Still, making new friends isn't always easy. As adults, we often have a more difficult time meeting new people because of the increased demands placed on us by work, family, and life overall. Most of us simply don't have the time to devote 20 hours a week to a flourishing social life.

We also don't have as many built-in opportunities for making friends as we did in childhood. As kids, we were surrounded by gaggles of potential playmates at school, sports programs, and summer camp. Often, making a new friend was as easy as walking over to the other kid on the playground and asking, "You like playing on the swings? Me too!"

But as adults, these built-in opportunities wane. This is not to mention that over the past several years, the number of people working from home and connecting over social media (instead of in person) has left many of us feeling socially anxious or awkward. I remember the first outdoor barbecue I attended after the lockdown days of the pandemic. It felt like a middle-school dance. And, of course, Nelson didn't make things easier for me:

Liz: I should go talk to my neighbor.

Nelson: What are you even going to say? All you have been
    doing for months is working, folding laundry, and making
    peanut butter and jelly sandwiches for your kids!

Liz: So what? She's been doing the same thing!

Nelson: Quick, think up some TV series you've watched so you
    can have a topic of conversation. Wait, that's boring and all
    anyone talks about right now.

Liz: But I don't know what else to talk about! Maybe I'll just go
    inside and go to the bathroom.

NELSON: You're going to sound like a doofus. You sound like this: "I like shows. You like shows? I eat food sometimes. You eat food too? I like soup."

LIZ: I'm not that bad, Nelson.

(Cut to me doing my best to chat with my neighbors like we hadn't been in our own little personal bunkers for months.)

I haven't done a scientific poll, but I feel confident that everyone sometimes feels socially anxious. This topic comes up with my clients all the time. Fortunately, here are some steps you can take to break the ice and reach out.

Monitor Your Internal Reactions and Self-Talk

Remember that chapter on the mind-body connection? Talking to someone new can activate your sympathetic nervous system, causing those anxious jitters that can make socializing seem like an insurmountable task. Remember to breathe, ground yourself in the present moment, and use positive affirmations like "I can do challenging things" and "I'm giving myself the opportunity for connection."

Acknowledge Any Shame or Embarrassment

If you feel apprehensive about talking to new people, it can bring up complicated feelings like shame and embarrassment. It can prompt negative thoughts like "Why can't I be more social?" or "What's wrong with me?" Nothing is wrong with you. Our world is not set up to prioritize in-person interactions anymore. You are not alone in feeling this way. You are a majestic, unique unicorn of a human being, so get out there and show off your awesomeness!

Practice Talking to New People

I don't mean putting yourself in unsafe or sketchy situations. Challenge yourself to connect with someone as you go about your daily life. Ask someone at the gas station for directions instead of figuring it out yourself. If you see an exceptionally stylish person, compliment them on their outfit or shoes. Chat with the server or barista that goes the extra mile to give you excellent service. Do something nice for your elderly neighbor and talk with them for a few minutes. The more you strike up conversations with new people, the easier it will become.

Find Common Ground

Talking to others will be much easier if you identify some common interests. Take a moment to reflect on the places where you feel most comfortable being your authentic self. Are you into comic books, contemporary art, sports, knitting, or Middle Eastern cooking? Use that information to intentionally find events and environments where you can meet other like-minded individuals. Knowing ahead of time that you have similar interests will make starting conversations less intimidating.

Embrace the Discomfort

It's okay if you don't feel totally comfortable talking with someone or the interaction doesn't go as smoothly as you would like. The point is to celebrate that you are getting out there! Keep practicing, and it will get easier, I promise. And even if the worst *does* happen, and the interaction *is* truly awkward, would it matter in a day, a week, a month, or a year?

This Is Your Brain on Love

After putting yourself out there and being among people for a while, you may meet someone who makes your heart race. And before you know it, you are in L-O-V-E. Romantic love feels intense, and there is a biochemical reason for that. When you fall for someone, your brain produces more dopamine, which is a hormone associated with reward and pleasure. Physical touch also leads to the production of oxytocin, the cuddle and love hormone that plays a huge role in bonding and attachment. It's for these reasons that romantic love is addicting. It leaves you coming back for more. It's no wonder that so many movies, songs, books, poems, and works of art all focus on desire. Some people would even say that being in love is like being high on cocaine. I've never tried cocaine, but I like to imagine it's similar to the carrot cake at Ted's Bulletin in Washington, DC.

Since romantic love can be so addicting, it's only natural that most of us have ignored a giant red flag (or 10) in our prior relationships. When you are desperate to make a relationship work, it's easy to ignore red flags. You tell yourself that this person will change or that it's not that bad. Fixer-uppers might be great buys in real estate, but when it comes to your love life and friendships, you deserve someone who is move-in ready.

Red flags in relationships are signals that you need to pause and evaluate your partner's behavior. Are their actions something you can live with over the long term? You are the expert on your own life, so ultimately, you have to decide who is and is not a right fit for you. These are a few examples of behavior that are cause for concern. These examples are not an exhaustive list of everything that could be a red flag in a relationship, so if you are unsure whether something is a sign of unhealthy behavior, ask yourself how you would feel if your best friend were treated in this manner. What if your teenager or adult child were being treated this way? If you would take offense to your best friend or child being subjected to this behavior, you should reflect on why it's acceptable for you to be treated this way.

Alcohol or Drug Use Is Negatively Interfering with Their Life

It is not someone's fault if they are dealing with substance abuse or addiction. Addiction is a disease that impacts the brain. Still, they must take responsibility for their behaviors. It's similar to someone who has type 1 diabetes. While it is not their fault that they have diabetes, it is still their responsibility to manage this health condition by taking medication and making necessary lifestyle changes. Healthy boundaries are essential if you are dating someone who is not taking responsibility for their substance use. You may decide to limit or avoid contact with that person until they develop healthier coping skills and stabilize their life. There are resources out there for friends and family of individuals with alcohol or substance use disorders, such as Al-Anon, Nar-Anon, and the Substance Abuse and Mental Health Services Administration.

They Have Aggressive or Violent Tendencies

My friend Stewart once dated a woman named Alana for a few months. It went well initially. They both liked Marvel films and swing dancing. But as time went on, Alana started to develop jealous feelings. Stewart would return from an office happy hour, and she would pepper him with questions about who was there and whom he talked to. She became convinced that Stewart was developing feelings for one of his coworkers. Now, Stewart is a tax attorney and is way more into numbers and the tax code than illicit office romances. Although he tried to communicate this to Alana, he couldn't convince her.

One evening, Alana picked up a slice of freshly delivered pizza and angrily threw it at Stewart in a fit of jealousy. Suffice it to say, Stewart decided, wisely, to end the relationship then and there. A person who deals with their emotions in this way—by becoming aggressive or violent—lacks empathy and doesn't have enough positive outlets for coping with the stress of life. You could be putting your safety (and the safety of your loved ones) at risk by engaging in relationships with aggressive or violent people. If Alana could throw a slice of pizza, what might she throw next?

You Have Different Priorities or Values

It can be challenging to sustain a long-term relationship if you and your partner are on different pages regarding what you want out of life. Perhaps you are positive that you want to have kids, but your partner is adamant that they don't want to be a parent. Maybe you love living in the city, but your partner can't see themselves settling down anywhere other than a ranch in Montana. Two good people can have fundamental differences that obstruct long-term commitment. Don't pretend to be okay with something if you really aren't. Although you and your partner do not have to be carbon copies—it's okay, even healthy, to have your own interests and preferences—make sure you are on the same page about the big stuff (e.g., kids, religion, where you will live, how you spend money) before making a long-term commitment.

They Don't Have Any Friends or Community

If your partner lacks any friendships or connections other than you, you may want to inquire about why this is. Humans are tribal people. Even the most introverted among us need connection. If someone does not put energy into their relationships, is closed off to others, or lacks the motivation to invest in their personal growth, this could create problems later on. That person may start looking at you to be their whole world, leaving you feeling tired or resentful. In relationships, both individuals need to develop their own sense of self. While you certainly want to have shared priorities and values as we just discussed, you also want to have your own interests, friends, and goals.

They "Bread Crumb" You

Bread crumbing involves being led on by another person. This person might show occasional interest by texting you at random intervals, sliding into your DMs on social media, or offering sporadic plans to meet up without consistent follow-through. Why do exes have that sixth sense to text "U up?" just as you are getting on with your life and doing great? Nothing is worse than someone offering just enough contact to make it hard for you to get over them. But here is the hard truth: If someone wants to be in a relationship with you, they will be. If someone constantly lets you down without a solid reason, that person is not making you a priority. You deserve someone who isn't leading you on. If someone is bread crumbing you, speak up and address the inconsistent communication so you can decide how to move forward. If you hear more from your local member of Congress asking you to vote in the next election than you hear from your boo, reevaluate the relationship.

They Show Toxic Behaviors Like Dishonesty, Jealousy, Control, and Gaslighting

It will be challenging, if not impossible, to develop an authentic connection with someone who constantly lies to you. Healthy relationships require trust. An insecure partner will often be jealous and question your interactions with others. They might try to control whom you see, what you wear, how you spend your money, what you post online, what you eat, how you exercise, or how you spend your time. They may also try to gain the upper hand in the relationship by gaslighting you with misinformation and making you question your reality, memory, and perceptions. The actions and words of a gaslighter can be confusing and disorienting. If you notice these toxic behaviors occurring, think carefully about whether or not you want to invest time and energy in this relationship.

They Treat Other People with Disrespect or Rudeness

If the person you are dating is a jerk to others, chances are they will also be cruel to you. Make sure to pay close attention to how they treat others, especially service workers. When you are at a restaurant, do they treat waitstaff with courtesy? Are they respectful of Uber drivers? Known as "The Waiter Rule," this provides vital information about their character. It will also serve you well to listen to how your partner talks about other people in their life. Are they always the victim? Is everyone else always the jerk? If they don't seem to like or get along with anyone, you may want to take a closer look at why that is and ask yourself if this relationship is worth continuing.

Related to the concept of disrespect and rudeness, if someone constantly trashes their "crazy" ex or refuses to talk about their previous relationships, you have reason to be wary. Not only does this reflect their inability to take responsibility for their role in the relationship ending, but they may also lack the skills to be an emotionally mature partner with you.

They Lack the Ability to Self-Reflect and Accept Responsibility

If your partner cares more about winning every argument with you than finding a resolution and preserving the relationship, you are in for a long and exhausting road ahead. For example, one of my clients, Elsie, was having difficulty parenting her oldest middle-school child, who had been acting out and even got suspended. She kept trying to get her husband,

Kevin, on the same page in providing consistent discipline, but he never followed through with the behavioral suggestions from the school.

One night, Elsie was at her wit's end. She tried to talk with Kevin, but he was far from sober after having consumed a few stiff cocktails earlier during happy hour. They ended up having a huge fight and talking in circles while Kevin dug in his heels. The next day, Kevin bought Elsie her favorite dessert, a red velvet cupcake, and in the following weeks, Elsie noticed that he started to manage their eldest's behavior better. But he didn't apologize to her. He didn't take responsibility for the role that alcohol played in their painful argument, nor did he explain why he was initially so defensive and resistant to trying new parenting techniques.

Kevin seemed to want Elsie to move on as if the argument had never happened. Elsie felt unheard and unacknowledged, and when she eventually communicated these feelings to Kevin, he ultimately did apologize. Still, a lot of pain would have been spared if he had been more willing to self-reflect, accept responsibility for his actions, and actively work to repair the relationship. In a healthy relationship, conflict isn't "me against you"—it's "us against a challenge." If your partner won't reflect on their behavior or accept responsibility for their role in a situation, repairs to the relationship will be difficult, if not impossible.

The Criteria for Trust

A relationship is like a house, with trust as the foundation that builds genuine connection and love. When you trust someone, you feel a sense of security with them. You are confident that they have your best interests at heart and will not try to harm you. For example, when you share the details of your life, like the downsizing you are facing at work or the scary news you've received about the health of a parent, you trust that they will keep this information safe instead of spreading it to the whole world. Or when you divulge some of your deepest and rawest emotions, you trust that they will make space for what you're feeling instead of dismissing or downplaying your experience. This type of trust is built over time through small actions and gestures.

But how can you tell if the person you are dating or the new friend you met at book club is trustworthy? I first knew I could trust my friend and neighbor Jess when I was on a weekend trip with my neighbors and kids. My youngest was having a colossal tantrum because, unbeknownst to me, she wanted to be the one to find the rainbow ball, and I accidentally found it first. Clearly, that made me a monster and the worst parent ever.

The meltdown went on for a good 45 minutes, after which I sank down to the floor and started crying too. Here I was, a freaking therapist who is supposed to be able to roll with anything, and my four-year-old had left me feeling discombobulated. At this point, Jess came in. She told me I was doing a great job and validated how hard these meltdowns can be. Nonjudgmental support from another parent was precisely what I needed in that moment. And I could trust that Jess had my back.

Trusting others can be especially hard if you haven't had a lot of role models for healthy relationships in your life or if your trust has been betrayed. I like to go by the five components of trust developed by Drs. John and Julie Gottman, who founded the Gottman Institute, an organization that has researched couples and families for the past five decades. They have done incredible work in many areas. These are their five criteria for trust in relationships:[15]

1. **Honesty:** Someone who lies to you cannot be trusted. Do not justify or make excuses for a dishonest person. If a guy says on his dating profile that he is in his mid-30s, and later you find out that he's closer to celebrating the big 5-0, you need to question why he wasn't up-front about this information. Do

you really want to be with someone who is fine with starting off the relationship on false pretenses?

2. **Transparency:** A trustworthy person will be open with you about their life. They will want you involved in their world. If you have been pals with someone for six months and you haven't met any of their family, friends, or coworkers, that should give you pause.

3. **Accountability:** A trustworthy person will keep their commitments and promises to you. If someone says they are going to call you at 8:30 p.m., they keep their word. And if for some reason they don't—let's say they got a flat tire on the way home—they let you know why.

4. **Ethical action:** If your values and morals do not align with someone, that person is not a good match for you. Ask yourself, *Do I respect this person's character?* and use that as a guide. If you're not down with someone who feels the urge to flip off every other driver on the interstate, maybe they're not right for you.

5. **Proof of alliance:** Proof of alliance occurs when you have each other's best interests at heart. You show up for each other in small and large ways. You know your friend or partner has your back. That middle-of-the-night phone call you make when you need help? You know they'll pick up.

It's tempting to go headfirst into a new relationship when you feel a spark or connection, but the wisest course of action is to make sure you can trust the other person first. When the prince asked Cinderella to marry him after a few dances at the ball, she should have said, "Hey, buddy, I appreciate your enthusiasm, but let's go for coffee first." Cinderella needed to find out if the prince showed up on time for dates, recycled his soda cans, and was nice to animals before locking things down permanently.

Dr. Helen Fisher, an anthropologist and human behavior researcher, also suggests waiting at least two years before marrying someone.[16] This allows for early, intense romantic feelings to subside (i.e., when your brain is lit up like fireworks and feels like it's high on cocaine) and gives you essential insight into how your partner handles holidays, the change in seasons, busy periods of work, and so forth. You might find that your own Prince Charming has a gambling problem that he hasn't been completely forthright about or that he spends too much of his time mansplaining cryptocurrency to you. By slowing down and dating thoughtfully, you give yourself a chance to see if a new person meets the criteria for trust. You then simultaneously build trust as you each become more emotionally invested in the relationship. This might not be as exciting as the plot of a Disney princess movie, but you are giving love a chance for the long haul.

The same goes for your friendships. You might meet someone and think they are the bee's knees: "Yes, this is the bestie I have been waiting for!" It's fantastic that you have found an exciting, new connection. But keep in mind that you will have to get to know their character and trustworthiness over time. Don't hand over any state secrets or give them the keys to your apartment until you know you can count on them, okay?

Getting Attached: The Four Attachment Styles

Your attachment style reflects how you interact with other people in your relationships. You form your attachment style based on your experiences with your caregivers growing up. Ideally, as a child, you had a caregiver or parent who was emotionally available and attuned to your needs. You learned that the world is, by and large, a safe place and that people, in general, can be trusted. You felt comfortable going out into and freely exploring the world because you had a safe person to rely on and return to.

On the other hand, your view of the world and relationships may have been skewed if you grew up in a household with a parent or caregiver who was emotionally unavailable, unresponsive to your needs, or mentally or physically abusive. As a child, you learned to see the world as uncertain and unsafe, leading to difficulty trusting others. This perspective often follows you into adulthood and causes difficulties in interpersonal relationships.

Individuals generally develop one of four attachment styles in response to these early experiences: secure, anxious, avoidant, or disorganized. Secure attachment represents the healthiest form of attachment, while anxious, avoidant, and disorganized all represent unhealthy attachment styles.

Secure Attachment

Individuals with a secure attachment style can be independent and build relationships with others. Children form this attachment style when they grow up with a safe base from which they can explore the world. As adults, people with this attachment style can ask for what they need and make repairs to their relationships after a conflict. A securely attached individual is aware of their partner's feelings. They can self-soothe and regulate their own emotions.

On the television show *The Office*, Jim and Pam demonstrate the qualities of a securely attached couple even though they have their ups and downs, just like any relationship. Their feelings for each other developed over time. They both pursue their own interests—Pam likes drawing and participating in art shows, while Jim plays practical jokes, like putting his coworker's stapler in Jell-O—and have friends outside of their relationship. They trust and look out for each other.

Anxious Attachment

A child can develop an anxious attachment style if they grew up in an environment where their parent or caregiver was inconsistent and sent mixed signals when responding to the child's needs. One moment the parent may have doted on the child, and the next they may have been emotionally unavailable. As adults, individuals with an anxious attachment style crave intimacy and fear abandonment, so they constantly monitor their relationships for any perceived signal of withdrawal. They are extremely worried about being cheated on and feel incapable of taking care of themselves, so they frequently seek reassurance regarding their partner's affection and commitment. They also tend to act out when they're feeling insecure about the relationship, for example, by calling or texting incessantly or by going over the top with gifts or grand gestures.

A fictional character that I suspect of having an anxious attachment style is Miss Piggy from *The Muppet Show*. She is desperate for Kermit's attention and constantly seeks reassurance about their relationship. Her jealous streak is so intense that she will even use karate to scare off anyone who threatens to interfere with her and Kermit. I'm fairly certain that if Miss Piggy had a cell phone, she would be constantly texting Kermit and also posting elaborate TikTok dances featuring her and her frog dressed in pink sequins and feathers.

Avoidant Attachment

Avoidant attachment is marked by a fear of intimacy and close relationships. Children can develop this attachment style if they grew up with parents or caregivers who were dismissive and emotionally distant. Individuals with an avoidant attachment style value their independence and dislike relying on people for support because they believe others will let them down. They also tend to be out of touch with their emotions and resist making compromises in relationships. A person with an avoidant attachment style might say things like "This relationship is moving too fast" or "You can't depend on anyone but yourself."

I've watched a lot of *Sesame Street* in my day due to being a parent of two tiny humans. Oscar the Grouch, holding court from his trash can, is the very definition of avoidant attachment. He rarely accepts help and is leery of developing bonds with any of his neighbors. Another example of avoidant attachment is Samantha Jones from *Sex and the City*. She is fiercely independent and successful but often has a hard time being vulnerable, accepting support from partners, and connecting on an emotional level in romantic relationships.

Disorganized Attachment

Disorganized attachment can result when a child is raised in an environment that is hostile, chaotic, or even abusive. Individuals with a disorganized attachment style may have received mixed messages from their caregivers while growing up, ranging from supportive and calming to harsh and mocking. This confusion leads them to both desire and fear connection. As adults, individuals with a disorganized attachment style have chaotic, unpredictable, and intense relationships. They want to be close to others but have difficulty when it comes to trust, so they push people away when connection overwhelms them. People with disorganized attachment feel intense discomfort being alone and have a tendency to end up in toxic relationships.

The character Rebecca Bunch in the TV series *Crazy Ex-Girlfriend* is an example of disorganized attachment. She quickly falls hard in both her friendships and romantic relationships, even quitting her job in New York and moving across the country to West Covina, California, on a whim for the chance at love. She goes back and forth between fearing that her relationships will end and pushing people away with over-the-top behavior.

How to Develop Secure Attachment

If you recognize yourself as having an unhealthy attachment style, rest assured! You are not doomed. You can form healthier relationships with others through awareness, self-reflection, and mindfulness. Simply being aware of the different attachment styles and identifying your own style can help you approach relationships in new ways. Journaling or discussing your relationships in therapy can help you develop insight too. You can also learn to validate yourself through positive self-talk and affirmations, as opposed to seeking reassurance from other people. The mindfulness and emotional regulation strategies I discussed in earlier chapters can help you sit with and tolerate intense and uncomfortable emotions, allowing you to be less reactive and think more clearly.

My client Larisa had an anxious attachment style when I first started working with her. She often worried when her boyfriend didn't text her back immediately, and her mind would spiral into thoughts like "He must be out with someone else" or "He doesn't really care about me." This caused her to check in frequently with him to make sure that everything was okay. Not surprisingly, she identified that past partners had often labeled her as "needy." In therapy, Larisa learned how to reframe her negative thoughts, use mindful breathing, and distract herself with fun activities when her boyfriend was out with friends to reduce her urge to check in with him excessively throughout the evening.

Love Languages

Gary Chapman developed the concept of the five "love languages" to describe how people give and receive affection in different ways. When you understand your love language, you can better communicate how you want to receive affection from the important people in your life. You can also better support your loved ones by showing them affection in the manner that suits them best. Not only will understanding the concept of love languages help you establish realistic expectations in relationships, but you'll have a greater sense of appreciation when your partner makes efforts to satisfy your wants and needs.

1. **Acts of service:** A person whose love language is acts of service appreciates it when their partner does practical tasks to make their life easier, whether it's putting gas in the car, finishing that tax paperwork, or handling a dreaded errand. To explain love languages in practice, let's use the food that unites us all—which, naturally, is tacos. An act of service could be picking up your partner's taco order from the restaurant down the street.

2. **Words of affirmation:** Individuals who value words of affirmation appreciate it when others share kind thoughts ("I like spending time with you"), give them compliments ("You are fun to be around"), or simply say, "I love you." Writing notes or letters is another way to affirm someone with words. Returning to tacos again, you could use words of affirmation by telling your partner, "I feel so cared for when you pick up my taco order and make sure they didn't forget the spicy salsa."

3. **Physical touch:** Individuals who value physical touch enjoy feeling the close presence of others in a nonverbal way. This can involve any safe form of physical connection, such as hugging, sitting close to someone, holding hands, or giving a back rub. When it comes to tacos, an example of physical touch would be giving your partner a giant hug when they arrive home after picking up your taco order.

4. **Quality time:** A person whose love language is quality time values spending uninterrupted and undivided time with their partner. This might look like going out on a date, taking a walk outside, running errands, or engaging in a hobby together. Taking time to give your partner your full attention during conversations (ahem, please put away your phone) can promote this love language as well. As applied to tacos, you can spend quality time sitting with your partner on your patio and eating the tacos they just brought home.

5. **Thoughtful gifts:** Finally, some people feel most loved when they receive thoughtful gifts. A gift does not have to be expensive or fancy for it to "count." It's all about the meaning behind the gift. A thoughtful gift shows that you know the other person well and are thinking about them. Remembering and celebrating special occasions and anniversaries is another way to express this love language. An example of a thoughtful gift could be surprising your partner with tacos and getting the guac and queso even though that's extra.

Taylor Tomlinson, a comedian, says that your love language "is whatever your partner *isn't* fucking doing right now." She has a point. If you are feeling unappreciated by your partner, what would help? Does your partner show you affection in ways you may have overlooked? For example, if you would be overjoyed if your girlfriend hugged you after a long day, ask for it! If you feel frustrated that your boyfriend never brings you flowers, but he always fills up your gas tank, can you begin to see some romance and affection in that action? Communicate your love languages to your partner and develop a greater appreciation for your partner's contributions. However, if your partner isn't showing any love languages, that could signify that you both are disconnected. Are there opportunities to reconnect, or do you need to reevaluate if this relationship is worth staying in?

You can also sustain long-term attachment and maintain feelings of romantic love by following some of these simple tips:

1. Seek out novel and exciting experiences with your partner. This could be anything from trying a new cuisine, traveling to a new place, attending a concert, or going bungee jumping together. Novelty releases dopamine (the reward and pleasure hormone) in the brain, which helps you feel more committed and positive toward your partner.

2. Have sex and embrace the power of physical touch—hold hands, cuddle, and give each other back rubs—to promote oxytocin (the love and cuddle hormone) and increase feelings of attachment. Being affectionate outside of the bedroom tends to lead to more connection in the bedroom too. (Wink, wink.)

3. Have empathy to see things from your partner's perspective. This is essential for effective problem-solving and conflict resolution. (I'll discuss how to practice active listening and navigate conflict in greater detail later in the chapter.)

4. Say kind things to your partner. It's important to continually validate that you have your partner's back and they have yours. And everyone wants to feel wanted and appreciated!

5. Lean into positive illusions. In other words, focus on your partner's positive qualities and overlook their flaws. Hey, maybe your partner does chew with their mouth open on occasion or has weird taste in music, but they do always take the dog out when it's 10 o'clock at night and you're too warm and cozy to get up from the couch. It might be worth it to forgive those funky little quirks in light of all the wonderful things they do. (Note: This does not mean you should tolerate abusive or toxic behavior. See the previous section on red flags!)

Rethinking the Fantasy of Soulmates

The idea of having a soulmate sounds so sexy and intense. Soulmates are the stuff of poetry, art, and great love stories. There is something so attractive about the idea that there is one perfect person out there that gets you on a deep, intimate, and spiritual level. I am about to be a total buzzkill right now, but you should give up the idea of a soulmate. Or, at the very least, rethink what having a soulmate means.

The problem with believing that someone is your soulmate is that it puts that person on a pedestal. It holds them to an impossible standard. You come to expect that they "should" know what you think and feel. That they "should" anticipate your wants and needs. This contributes to breakdowns in communication, leaving you feeling let down when they buy you a three-pack of car washes for your birthday when you had hoped for a romantic dinner or a shiny piece of jewelry. But remember that your partner is only human. I've said it before, and I'll say it again: Humans are not perfect. The human condition is delightfully flawed and messy.

Another problem is that you're more likely to become codependent on your partner when you view them as a soulmate. You begin to consider yourself and your partner as a unit instead of two inter-connected individuals. You lose sight of your own uniqueness and interests. It becomes harder to function without them. You start to depend on them for companionship, entertainment, emotional support, stability, and financial security. You might even downplay or enable behavior that could be a red flag or deal-breaker. Maybe you notice that your partner gets angry when they drink. Or perhaps you've caught them lying. It can be easy to brush unacceptable behavior like this under the rug if you are committed to the fantasy that this person is your one true love.

I like to think that many people in this world are my soulmates. The universe brings people into my life for various reasons. These relationships may last a lifetime or only a short time, but all these connections are meaningful. Every relationship can teach you something important. I also think you can be your own soulmate. Your relationship with yourself is the first and last relationship you will ever have. You have to love yourself before you can love someone else. If you don't care about yourself, you won't feel worthy of someone else's love.

Suffice it to say, I would really make a shitty Hallmark movie script writer. In my perfect romantic movie, two people would meet each other in a safe and well-lit public location during the day, like a coffee shop or the zoo. These two individuals would take their time getting to know each other and build trust before becoming physically intimate. They would introduce each other to their friends and family. They would go to concerts or make grilled cheese and tomato soup. On the weekends, they'd go hiking and visit flea markets. They get on each other's nerves occasionally but talk it out. They'd regularly pursue their own interests and socialize with their own friends. Although this isn't the exciting and dramatic stuff movies are made of, it's sane, safe, and beautiful. This is my kind of romance.

The Fine Art of Listening

All human beings want to be heard. When someone takes the time to listen to you and truly understand your perspective, it is a validating experience. Likewise, giving someone your full attention and making them your top priority, even for a few moments, is an incredible gift. Taking the time to listen, whether it's to a friend, partner, coworker, or neighbor, can help prevent misunderstandings, deepen relationships, and leave a positive and lasting impression.

Being a good listener requires being present in the moment. Unfortunately, in our fast-paced and multitasking culture, being present is usually not on our priority list. Most of us are busy texting, watching the news, heating up a slice of pizza, petting the dog, and waiting to switch the laundry into the dryer all at the same time.

One way to become more present in your conversations with others is to practice active listening. Active listening involves working to understand the entire message the speaker is trying to get across rather than just simply hearing the words they are saying. It seems obvious in theory, but it is powerful in practice. Active listening is a technique I use every day as a therapist. It lets my clients know that I am paying attention to them and that I value what they are saying. Here are a few steps you can take to practice active listening in your life.

Step 1: Focus on what the other person is saying.
It might sound simplistic, but we often don't listen to what other people are saying because we're too busy figuring out what intelligent and witty comment we want to say next. Our thoughts might also be drifting to what we want for lunch or what's left on our to-do list. Active listening requires you to be in the moment and pay special attention to the speaker's verbal *and* nonverbal messages. Give the speaker your full attention by making good eye contact, nodding along to demonstrate that you are engaged, and encouraging them to continue by using brief statements like *yes* and *uh-huh*.

Resist the temptation to get distracted by side conversations or background noise, and avoid mentally planning your rebuttal. Suspend any judgments you may have about the other person's thoughts, and resist the urge to interrupt, immediately give advice, or offer counterarguments. Interrupting the speaker conveys that what you have to say is more important. Interruption can also be contagious. When you cut someone off, they will be more likely to do the same in return since you didn't offer them the courtesy of allowing them to complete their thought.

Step 2: Reflect on the speaker's words and relay their message back to them.

Once the other person is finished talking, ask yourself what you think the speaker was trying to convey to you. What did the person want you to take away from their comments? Perhaps you notice that your friend, Simone, is frowning and furrowing her brow when discussing the difficulties she's experienced at her new job. Using this information, you want to either paraphrase or mirror the speaker's message back to them in your own words using phrases like "What I'm hearing you say is . . ." or "It sounds like . . ." For example, you could say to Simone, "It sounds really frustrating to have to learn so much so fast." Avoid parroting the person's exact words too much because that can quickly get annoying.

Step 3: Ensure that you have accurately heard the speaker.

The next step is to check your reflection for accuracy by asking the speaker if what you heard was correct. You might follow up your comment by saying, "Am I understanding that correctly?" or "Did I get that right?" This gives the speaker a chance to either correct your initial assumption or continue the conversation. For example, Simone might respond, "No, I am not frustrated with the workload. The problem is that my coworker doesn't communicate well." Or she might say, "Yes, I am overwhelmed with everything I have to learn."

Step 4: Continue the conversation by returning to step 1 or asking clarifying questions.

At this point, you will either continue following the previous set of steps or ask clarifying questions that solicit additional information, such as "Can you tell me more about what you meant when you said . . . ?" or "Did you mean that . . . ?" Whenever you're in doubt, make sure to clear up any ambiguities by asking questions instead of assuming you know what the other person is thinking or feeling.

And no matter what, resist jumping in with solutions. We've all had that experience when we are trying to talk about something tough and the other person says, "Well, why don't you just . . . ?" or "Here's what I would do." It feels deflating and frustrating. We often pressure ourselves to fix other people's problems, but that is not the goal of active listening. Active listening is about making the other person feel understood and supported. The goal is to be empathetic rather than dismissive. You want to let the other person know that you genuinely see their perspective and are there for them. Empathetic phrases sound like "That sounds tough" or "How can I best support you?" This is in contrast to being dismissive, in which you invalidate the other person and imply that you are trying to "fix" them. Dismissive language sounds like "Other people have it worse" or "This isn't a big deal." By giving the other person a chance to talk and feel heard, they can often come up with solutions and conclusions on their own.

I used active listening recently when I talked to my client Sofia about the relationship she has with her dad:

SOFIA: I don't like spending time with my dad anymore. He is always asking me a million questions about my life.

LIZ: It sounds like you feel like you are being interrogated.

SOFIA: Yeah, it's exhausting. I'd just like to call him without feeling like I need to give a full report on my life.

LIZ: You want your conversations with him to feel more relaxed. Did I get that right?

SOFIA: That's it. Sometimes I only have the energy for a quick check-in. And there are times when I just want to talk about everyday stuff, like what I watched on Hulu, as opposed to who I am dating and my grades in law school.

Liz: It sounds like you feel your dad is checking up on you sometimes in your conversations. Is that the case?

Sofia: No, I don't feel like he is checking up on me. He knows I am on top of everything, but I feel like he just cares about my accomplishments and not about me as a person.

Liz: That sounds hard. You want your relationship with your dad to be more than just your accomplishments.

Sofia: Yes.

You will be amazed at how great you can make someone feel just by listening to what they are saying, reflecting back what you've heard, and taking the time to understand their perspective. Try it out the next time you're interacting with an angry team member or customer and watch them instantly become calmer. You might even thwart the next geopolitical conflict! Or, at the very least, it will help you build goodwill with your coworkers and friends.

And one final note: Don't underestimate the power of asking others what they need from you when you're not sure. In other words, inquire if they are seeking a solution or support. If your best friend is talking about a problem she has at work, ask her if she wants help with problem-solving or wants you to listen. You don't have to fix other people's issues to be supportive.

Fight Fair

Relationships don't have to be perfect to be long-lasting. And in fact, they won't be. All relationships will inevitably experience conflict from time to time. This is normal. Humans are messy and complicated creatures. We do not always see eye to eye. Therefore, the secret to forming lasting relationships doesn't have to do with whether or not you will experience conflict. It's about figuring out how to navigate that conflict constructively.

Just like there are some ground rules in WrestleMania (no low blows, unauthorized props, chokeholds, or ripping off signature moves—and keep any dangly bits covered), there are a few guidelines to keep in mind when navigating conflict in relationships:

- Wait for your emotional reactivity to subside before you attempt to address the conflict. Take time to breathe, get some sleep, work out, or eat before having a difficult discussion. You don't want to start the conversation on the warpath.

- Discuss one issue at a time. It's going to be a long night if you try to address everything that has ever gone wrong in your relationship.

- Focus on solving the problem at hand rather than winning the argument.

- Don't put down the other person, call them names, or yell.

- Try to see things from the other person's perspective and understand why this particular issue might be triggering for them. For example, perhaps your partner is especially sensitive when it comes to spending money because they grew up in a financially insecure environment.

- Take a break if the conversation is getting too heated or if either person is under the influence of alcohol or mind-altering substances.

- Communicate assertively (like we addressed in the chapter on boundaries) using "I" statements. This might look like "I feel frustrated and disrespected when you leave dishes in the sink and I'm expected to clean up after you. In the future, please put your dishes in the dishwasher."

Apologize Like a Pro

In addition to navigating conflict constructively, a necessary part of maintaining lasting relationships is knowing how to make amends when a rupture does occur. Still, not all apologies are created equal. A genuine apology does not contain the word *but*. Sir Mix-a-Lot may have said, "I like big butts, and I cannot lie," but a big *but* has no place in a proper apology. Here I am referencing the tendency to say "I am sorry, but . . ." when attempting to make amends. We have all been on the receiving end of a quasi apology such as these:

- "I'm sorry I hurt your feelings, *but* you're too emotional."

- "I'm sorry, *but* I was just joking. Can't you take a joke?"

- "I didn't mean to hurt you, *but* you should know I've been stressed out."

- "I'm sorry you felt bad, *but* this isn't a big deal."

In all of these examples, the second part of the sentence negates the first. When you justify an apology with *but*, you are essentially telling the person you hurt that they shouldn't feel bad. You are sending the message that they are at fault because they are too sensitive and their emotions aren't valid. You are failing to take full responsibility for the harm you have caused.

When you make a genuine apology, you resist the urge to justify your behavior or provide excessive explanations. A heartfelt apology communicates that you understand what you did wrong. You take responsibility for your actions. A sincere apology also includes an acknowledgment of what you will do differently in the future. For example, if you forgot to pick up your roommate from work, you might say, "I am so sorry that I forgot to pick you up. I understand that I left you in a bind and you had to scramble to take an Uber. In the future, I will be better about checking my calendar before saying yes to a commitment." Mistakes happen, and that's okay. Just own it!

Action Items

1. Think about how you like to give and receive affection. What is your love language? What are the love languages of the other important people in your life?

2. Try active listening with a friend or loved one. What did it feel like? How did they respond?

3. Reflect on your previous relationships. What lessons did you learn from them? What red flags did you minimize or gloss over? What can you do differently in the future?

CHAPTER 7

EVERYONE'S GOT GRIEF

 The most beautiful people we have known are those who have known defeat, known suffering, known struggle, known loss, and have found their way out of the depths. These persons have an appreciation, a sensitivity, and an understanding of life that fills them with compassion, gentleness, and a deep loving concern. Beautiful people do not just happen.

—Elisabeth Kübler-Ross

The Definition of Grief

Our society tends to glorify good vibes, enthusiasm, happily ever after, and makeover stories. Think about all the fairy tales you read when you were a kid. The main character rides off into the sunset escorted by singing woodland creatures and a wealthy royal on their way to shack up in some magnificent castle. And practically every teen movie features someone who gets a new haircut and a cute outfit. Then they get crowned prom queen or king, and everything else falls into place before the credits roll.

I probably don't need to tell you this, but that's not how life works. Not all stories get a happy ending. The truth is that we will all have to deal with grief throughout our lives. And not to be a major Debbie Downer, but there is a 100 percent chance we will all die someday.

While it is possible to avoid feeling the pain of grief, that would require you to bypass love, connection, attachment, and everything that makes life worth living. The experience of grief means that you dared to love and care about someone or something. Therefore, learning how to sit with grief is a skill that everyone needs.

But what is grief exactly? It is a natural reaction to the loss or the anticipated loss of something you cherish. Losses can be tangible, like the physical loss of a person or home, or intangible, like a symbolic loss of aspirations or dreams. Grief also doesn't describe a single emotion. Instead, it encompasses a range of emotions, such as sadness, regret, guilt, anxiety, anger, numbness, and frustration (to name a few). Individuals experiencing grief often feel like they're on an emotional roller coaster, unsure of what will come next. That is entirely normal.

It's also important to note that grief is not a linear process, nor does it follow a specific timeline. Contrary to popular belief, grief does not fit into a set of prescribed stages like denial, anger, bargaining, depression, and acceptance. This chapter will discuss how to cope with and adjust to the complicated emotions that arise after loss.

Got Grief?

Oftentimes, people think that grief only happens after the death of a loved one, but grief can surface at many different times in life. We all have to navigate circumstances that involve changes, challenges, and endings, which can lead to feelings of loss. And anytime you experience both change and loss, you get grief. You might feel sorrow when you first go to college and have to say goodbye to your hometown and friends from high school. You might grieve over a job opportunity you didn't get or a romantic relationship that has come to an end. You might grieve when your beloved pet dies. Individuals who come out as LGBTQIA+ may feel grief when their parents or community refuse to accept their identity.

Some people are surprised when they experience grief following the death of a celebrity or influencer. The death of such a significant person brings up thoughts of our own mortality and reminds us that no one will be here forever. It challenges our sense of normalcy and security. It can also lead us to grieve the secondary losses resulting from that person's death, such as the loss of their creativity, their talent, and the pivotal role they played in society. For example, the death of U.S. Supreme Court Justice Ruth Bader Ginsburg was sad and painful to many. She was a trailblazer and feminist icon who fiercely protected race and gender equality, reproductive rights, and other fundamental liberties. Her death brought about feelings of fear and uncertainty. We worry how the absence of her leadership on the Supreme Court may have far-reaching implications on our individual lives and communities, especially in a political climate that feels increasingly polarized.

Many of my clients also often discuss the grief they can experience following the loss of a friendship or following changes to a friend group. It's common to assume that friendships are forever and will never change. But friendships do end when you grow apart, become separated by geography, or have changing priorities. That doesn't mean you have done anything wrong. I lost friendships during the political turmoil of the 2020 elections (let's just say I may have posted some strongly worded messages on social media). However, I realized those particular connections were rooted in going out and drinking copious amounts of wine rather than having shared values and emotional connections. But even when friendships end, those memories are still valid and important. A relationship doesn't have to last forever to be meaningful.

Between relationships and life transitions, we deal with loss more often than you would think. The following are all situations that can bring on grief:

- Illness or injury

- Estrangement, divorce, or separation

- The end of a friendship
- Being let down by a parent or caregiver
- Natural disasters
- A loved one who is struggling with alcohol or drug abuse
- Infertility or miscarriage
- Physical assault or sexual violence, or being the victim of a crime
- Incarceration of a loved one
- A relative who is experiencing dementia
- The experience of abuse or neglect
- Moving to a new community or immigrating to a new country
- The loss of identity after a major life event (e.g., having a baby, getting married, graduating)
- Working from home and losing connection to colleagues
- Financial insecurity
- Conflict between family or friends due to political, religious, or ideological differences

What's more, grief isn't just experienced on the individual level. We grieve as communities and as a society. The past several years have brought devastating news stories to our attention, from school shootings and riots, to natural disasters and economic uncertainty. The COVID-19 pandemic was a significant example of collective grief. The pandemic drastically altered everyone's way of life, practically overnight. Many grieved as they lost their daily routine, social connections, community activities, hobbies, financial security, and sense of safety. All those little daily and weekly rituals that never seemed very significant suddenly culminated in a considerable loss. Having lunch with your coworkers or visiting your grandmother every Thursday was no longer possible. The daily ritual of getting up, dressing up for work, and riding the subway was gone. The grief that resulted from these losses was genuine.

Society's Attitudes toward Grief and Loss

Unfortunately, our culture does not deal with grief and loss very well. People in the United States tend to be great at responding to crises in the moment but less helpful when offering long-term support. This can play out in big and small ways. For example, in the weeks and months following a large-scale crisis, such as a natural disaster, terrorist attack, or other humanitarian emergency, support often dwindles at the community level as the news cycle jumps to another topic. This can happen at a more individual level too. After the death of a parent, you may find yourself overwhelmed with flowers, noodle casseroles, and cards as friends and neighbors drop in to express their condolences. After a few weeks pass by, you feel increasingly alone in your grief as these sources of support slowly disappear.

You may feel this same dynamic play out after a breakup too. A month or two might pass following the dissolution of your relationship, yet you still acutely feel the loss. At this point, your friends and family have moved on, and they expect you to have done the same in turn. It can be tough to portray an image of everything being "all good" to the outside world when you feel anything but good internally. Seeing engagement notices or walking past your weekly brunch spot, even months later, can still trigger painful feelings.

Types of Grief

At this point in the chapter, you likely understand that grief is a complicated experience that can come in many different forms. You can feel relieved that a loved one is no longer suffering and still acutely feel their absence in your life. You can value the time you had with a person and feel like it wasn't enough. You can be hopeful about finding a new job after your company downsizes and still feel disappointed and anxious that your safety net has been taken away. You can feel more than one thing at a time, especially in grief. Understanding the different types of grief can help you better comprehend your reactions to loss.

Anticipatory Grief

Anticipatory grief occurs when you know that a loss is coming. Complicated emotions arise when you imagine a future beyond a significant life change or loss. You may be excited about graduation but sad that your friends will soon be spread out across the country. You can also experience anticipatory grief when you have a friend or loved one with a terminal illness. You know that their passing is inevitable, so the pain begins before their death occurs. Because anticipatory grief accompanies an impending loss, it can motivate you to take advantage of what you appreciate in the present moment. It can also prompt you to repair relationships, engage in meaningful experiences, spend time with loved ones, and take the time to say goodbye.

When my dad entered hospice care at home, the reality started to set in for me that he wasn't going to get better. I remember feeling awkward when people sent get-well cards and expressed their hopes for his recovery. While I appreciated my community's support, my gut knew that this was not a "Get well soon!" situation. I already felt the impact of anticipatory grief at that point.

Delayed Grief

Delayed grief is a grief reaction that appears seemingly out of nowhere, long after a death or loss occurred. Individuals in this situation may find themselves impacted by the loss when they least expect it. For example, after the death of a parent during a child's elementary school years, a teenager may find themselves overcome with grief years later when they realize that their loved one will be unable to attend their college orientation. I often find myself missing my dad when my kids say something funny, since my dad had such an irreverent sense of humor.

Delayed grief can also occur when someone has so much to manage after a significant loss that they cannot process their grief until life slows down or they have a greater sense of safety and stability. An executive might dive back into work shortly after losing all her belongings in a house fire as a way to distract herself from the uncomfortable feelings of grief. A child in foster care may not be able to process the death of a relative until they are in a stable home environment. These feelings of numbness or shock after a loss can be the brain's way of helping someone survive until they have the physical and emotional bandwidth to grieve.

Cumulative Grief

Cumulative grief, also known as "grief overload," occurs when someone experiences several significant losses within a short period of time. For example, someone might get furloughed from their job, only to find out two months later that they've been diagnosed with cancer and that their best friend is moving to a new city for work. Other people may have witnessed the death of several family members during the COVID-19 pandemic or as the result of a natural disaster.

Cumulative grief can also occur when a person has been using drugs or alcohol for an extended period of time to numb their pain and emotions. Once that person stops using, years of accumulated losses can surface simultaneously. Cumulative grief can lead people to lose their sense of safety and security. It can shake their worldviews, personal values, and spiritual or religious beliefs. If you are experiencing cumulative grief, reach out for support so you don't have to carry this emotional burden by yourself. This might look like going to therapy, attending a support group, finding a faith community, or letting your friends know you need extra TLC.

Disenfranchised Grief

Disenfranchised grief occurs when you experience a loss that is not recognized or accepted by your community or society at large. Because the loss is not understood or known publicly, you are alone in your grief. For example, during the AIDS epidemic, many in the LGBTQIA+ community experienced the deaths of their friends and partners but received no support due to the stigma surrounding the disease and the fact that many people were not out to their friends and families. They were unable to mourn publicly.

One of my clients is a teacher in a charter school. He was born and raised in the neighborhood surrounding the school, so he feels a deep sense of connection to the community. Unfortunately, the school has experienced several student deaths due to gun violence. While the community collectively grieves these losses, my client often feels alone in his grief. The deaths of his students do not garner much attention in the news and have not yet spurred any sweeping societal or policy change. His family and friends are supportive, but it's often hard for them to understand the emotional and longstanding impact of these deaths.

Other examples of disenfranchised grief can include:

- The death of a pet

- Deaths involving suicide or addiction

- The death or illness of a coworker, client or patient, or former romantic partner

- Miscarriage or infant loss

- An adoption that does not work out

- The loss of a foster child who is transferred or reunited with their biological family

- The loss of your home or job

- The death of a celebrity

- The death of a godparent

- The loss of a teacher or mentor

- The death of a nonprimary partner in a polyamorous relationship

- The loss of someone you didn't know, like an absent parent

- The death of someone with whom you used to be close

People going through disenfranchised grief typically don't receive any Hallmark cards or gift baskets as they mourn their loss. They often feel isolated because society does not acknowledge their grief as legitimate. Still, these losses are valid, and the pain they are experiencing is real.

Traumatic Grief

Traumatic grief results when the circumstances surrounding a loss are distressing, violent, preventable, or unexpected. This can include car accidents, natural disasters, suicide, or violence. Individuals experiencing traumatic grief may have symptoms of posttraumatic stress disorder, including intrusive thoughts or flashbacks, nightmares, anxiety, and changes in their sleep or appetite. They may become preoccupied with how their loved one died and harbor intense anger or guilt.

Most individuals who have experienced trauma do not want to or can't talk about what happened. If you have experienced traumatic loss, it's essential to attend to your trauma symptoms before focusing on grief. After a horrifying event, healing from traumatic grief requires regaining a sense of safety, trust, control, and identity. If your symptoms do not subside over time or are interfering with your day-to-day functioning, don't hesitate to check in with a mental health professional with experience in traumatic loss.

Complicated Grief

It is normal to feel devastated after the loss of a loved one. For most people, these acute feelings of pain and sadness improve with time. However, when these feelings remain intense long after the loss has occurred, someone is said to have complicated grief. Certain factors can make a person feel frozen in their grief. For example, during the COVID-19 pandemic, it was impossible for many to be with their loved ones when they died and engage in the normal rituals of mourning like funerals and memorial services. This made it difficult for grieving individuals to accept the reality of their loss and find support.

Although complicated grief resembles depression, it's not the same. A person experiencing complicated grief lacks hope that they can live a meaningful life without their loved one. They may be preoccupied with thoughts of the person who died and have difficulty thinking about anything else. Alternatively, they may go to great lengths to avoid reminders of their loss. These symptoms get in the way of daily life and can interfere with their ability to maintain healthy relationships. If this describes your experience, don't hesitate to find support through therapy, a support group, books, or other grief resources.

Pain versus Suffering

When it comes to grief, there is an essential difference between pain and suffering. Pain is an unavoidable part of the human experience and is a normal response to loss. Pain happens when you miss or long for something valued and cherished. Pain hurts because it means you dared to love and subsequently lost someone or something. Suffering, on the other hand, occurs when you or other people try to take away or deny your pain.

My inner critic, Nelson, used to make an appearance on a regular basis when I was grieving the death of my dad in high school. He would often make statements judging how I was grieving, which contributed to my suffering.

NELSON: You really need to quit being such a downer. No one is going to want to be friends with you if you don't act happy. Besides, your life isn't *that* bad. You have your basic needs covered. People brought casseroles. Scalloped potatoes for days! Mountains of mac and cheese! You should feel grateful for what you've got.

LIZ: Yeah, I get it. But what am I supposed to do? Fake being happy?

NELSON: Yeah, exactly. Pretend everything is great. Then you won't suck so much in show choir. You aren't smiling enough, and your jazz hands are lackluster. You're like Wednesday Addams in green sequins.

LIZ: Okay, fine, I'll try. I'll pretend to be happy.

NELSON: Good. Maybe then someone will ask you to the homecoming dance.

(Cut to me expending a ton of energy faking a smile and making sure I had perky jazz hands.)

You might also hear the following statements from your inner critic or from someone else in your life after a loss:

- "At least they are in a better place."
- "You can always find a new job."
- "You need to move on with your life."
- "You should be grateful for what you have."
- "You'll be able to have other kids."

- "At least you had so much time with your spouse."

- "They wouldn't want you to be sad."

- "Think positive."

- "Find the silver lining."

- "Other people have it worse."

Even though these statements can be well-intentioned, they seek to minimize or take away the pain. These types of comments fall under the umbrella of toxic positivity and send the message that you do not have a right to your own pain and sadness, all of which create suffering. I swear, if another stranger on the streets of Washington, DC, tells me to smile, I am going to slug them with my big ole mom purse. Sometimes people just don't feel like smiling or have a very good reason as to why they aren't feeling cheery, and that is perfectly okay.

Suffering also occurs when you try to take away your pain by doing things that numb you or bring about more stress in the long run. That might look like mindlessly scrolling through your phone or buying things you don't need. It can also look like gambling, drinking too much, forgetting to eat, spending time with people who drain your energy, or pretending like everything is okay when it's not.

With grief, the goal is to honor your pain while easing your suffering. You can do so by sitting with your pain, naming what you feel, and allowing yourself to feel these emotions. You can also relieve suffering by being intentional about what boundaries you set, whom you spend your time with, and how you care for yourself. You can ease your suffering by looking at what you can control and taking small actions in that direction. As grief expert and author Megan Devine explains, "Taking even the smallest action on your behalf to reduce suffering can bring back a little agency, a sense of personal power, inside a world that has turned upside down."[17]

Guilt versus Regret

Guilt has a way of sneaking in after a loss. Maybe you feel guilty about something you did or didn't say before someone died. Perhaps you question your actions in a relationship that ended. I often see this happen with clients who have experienced the death of a loved one by suicide. They feel guilty because they think they could have done something to prevent the death. They often replay the hours and days before the suicide. They question if an argument about loading the dishwasher or forgetting to make a phone call caused their loved one to die by suicide, but it's rarely that simple. There are many factors that can contribute to an individual dying by suicide, even if they had an abundance of resources, treatment, and community support. A death by suicide is not the fault of anyone. Also, to slide in a quick clarification (because language matters!), people don't *commit* suicide. People *die by* suicide. Suicide isn't a crime or a moral failing. It's an illness.

Although many people believe they are feeling guilt after the death of a loved one (by suicide or for any other reason), what they are actually feeling is regret. Guilt is the belief that you did something bad. It pertains to your actions and behaviors. You feel guilty when you intentionally act in a manner that does not align with your values. Conversely, regret is the knowledge that you could or would have done something different if you had more information at the time. For example, if you had known in advance that someone would die on a specific day, you might wish you could have told them "I love you" or taken the time to call or visit. But you didn't have that detailed information. None of us can predict the future. You did your best at that moment with whatever information you did or did not have.

For a long time, I carried a lot of guilt for the occasions when I was a bratty, snot-nosed kid around my dad. Part of me believed I should have anticipated his life being cut short and compensated for that by being a perfect child. But I eventually realized that all kids can be trying at times. That's just part of normal development. I can look back on this with the experience and maturity I have now and offer that younger version of myself some grace and understanding.

Adjusting to Loss

Grief sometimes feels like being homesick for a place that doesn't exist anymore. It hurts physically, mentally, emotionally, socially, and spiritually. If you are in the midst of grief, you may notice a lot of symptoms or just a few, including:

- Difficulties with concentration and memory

- Fatigue

- A wide range of emotions, such as sadness, irritability, anger, guilt, shock, and regret

- Changes in appetite (eating more or less than usual)*

- Changes in sleep quantity and quality (sleeping more or less than usual)

- Dreams or nightmares about the loss

- Increased isolation

- Not wanting to talk about the loss (or, conversely, telling the story of the loss over and over)

- Headaches or stomachaches

- Concern that someone else might die or that you might experience another loss

---

* Fun fact: The German word *kummerspeck* loosely translates into "grief bacon" or "sorrow fat" to describe the emotional eating that occurs after a difficult event or loss. Best word ever.

- Worries about the length and intensity of your grief (i.e., wondering if you are grieving the "right" way or being concerned that your pain isn't getting better)

- Questioning of your values, beliefs, and faith

Grief symptoms aren't pleasant, but they can be your brain's way of protecting you. Memory issues, brain fog, numbness, avoidance, and denial prevent you from being utterly consumed with the loss so you can process your emotions over time. While I wish I had a magic wand or foolproof formula to take the pain away, it's completely normal to experience these symptoms after a loss, and there are coping strategies that can help you feel better. The following are all strategies that I encourage you to try. Since everyone grieves differently, what works for one person may be less helpful for another, so take what works and leave the rest.

Give Yourself Permission to Feel

Grief can be complicated and confusing. You might feel sad, disappointed, angry, frustrated, lonely, resentful, betrayed, hurt, guilty, anxious, shocked, exhausted, or even relieved. (Just to name a few!) All of these emotions are valid and normal. No matter what you feel, you don't ever have to feel bad about feeling bad. In high school, after my dad died, I felt like an outcast, and Nelson would be hard on me for being the "sad kid." There weren't many emo cliques I could hang with in my small Illinois hometown, so I just ended up repeatedly playing Weezer's cover of "Teenage Dirtbag" on the car stereo. I would try to talk myself out of feeling down because I thought I wouldn't fit in with my classmates if I didn't radiate good vibes. But I had every right to be sad. And you have every right to feel whatever emotions surface for you.

Take Excellent Physical Care of Yourself

I'm no stranger to eating my feelings when I'm having a hard time. You've probably figured that out by the number of times I have referenced breakfast burritos, pizza, and nachos in this book. But that said, it is essential to take care of yourself following adversity. Don't add to your suffering by putting your body through the wringer. As tempting as it is to drown your sorrows with a bottle of wine, you will only feel worse the next day. Grief plus hangxiety is an express ticket for the pain train headed to suffering city. When your world has fallen apart, focus on the basics: Get sleep, drink water, eat regular meals, go outside, shower occasionally, brush your teeth, breathe, and move your body.

Ask for What You Need

When something shitty happens, friends and family often say, "Let me know what I can do." Although it's often tough to know what you need following a loss, if there is something that someone can do for you, ask! People genuinely do want to help, but they don't know how. If you want someone to hang out with you while you watch reruns of *30 Rock* and chow down on veggie lo mein, ask. If you dread a task like rewriting your resume or going through your mail, text your most organized friend for help.

Offer Yourself Grace and Patience

I'm going to give it to you straight. Following a loss, you aren't on your "A" game. That can be a real blow to your ego in a hustle culture that glorifies productivity. Grieving takes a lot of mental, physical, and emotional energy. As a result, it becomes a challenge to concentrate and focus. You may completely forget to attend a weekly meeting with your colleague, even though you are typically super organized. Maybe you leave a load of wet laundry in the washer for 72 hours, head out of the house with your shirt on backward, or drive home with your iced coffee on the roof of your car. That's normal. Be patient and try to take something off your plate if you can.

Avoid People and Situations That Drain Your Energy

Remember the previous chapter on healthy boundaries? You will need those following a loss to protect your precious emotional, mental, and physical energy. It's okay if you aren't up for that yearly football tailgate with your college friends. You can turn down an invitation from that auntie who complains about everything. If your best friend from college tends to dump on you emotionally, look for other sources of support. You have a limited amount of energy after a loss. Conserve your energy whenever possible and budget wisely.

Find Some Support

I used to run a grief and loss support group for tweens. Every week, a gaggle of 8-to-11-year-olds and I would drink lemonade and eat cookies in a conference room while we played games, did art projects, and talked about grief. Before the first session, the caregivers and parents nervously handed over their kids to me, likely fearing their child would shortly be overcome with sadness and despair. But that typically didn't happen. Once the kids understood that their fellow group members were like them and that everyone there was dealing with the significant death of a loved one, a sense of relief filled the room. It was like letting the air out of a balloon. I'll never forget when I overheard a conversation between one of my tweens and her mom after a group session. Her mom asked how it went, and the girl replied, "It was hilarious!" And it was true, we did laugh a lot. The kids trusted each other and had permission to laugh, cry, be mad, and feel whatever they felt.

I want you to find the same for yourself. Consider joining a formal support group, or look for other places where you might discover nonjudgmental and caring people. That could be a book club, an improv class, a faith community, a gym, a networking event for job seekers, or a volunteer organization. Volunteering after a recent loss or challenge can be a nice distraction, even (or especially) if the cause is unrelated to your circumstances. For example, suppose you had a friend recently die by suicide. You might find comfort in working with animals or at a community garden. That's not to say you couldn't eventually volunteer for a nonprofit organization working to prevent suicide, but you might need time to process your loss first.

Acknowledge the Secondary Losses

Secondary losses are those that follow a primary loss. It's the domino effect that occurs. An example of a primary loss is being laid off from your job after your company downsizes. The secondary losses that follow could include the loss of your professional identity, work community, routine, social outlets (the weekly office happy hour or softball game), financial security, and health care benefits. Some examples of other common secondary losses include the loss of your:

- Social status

- Faith

- Confidence and identity

- Financial stability

- Security

- Dreams and imagined future

- Daily routine

- Family structure

- Traditions

- Family history

- Support system

Often, secondary losses cause just as much pain and distress, and sometimes more, as the primary loss. These voids need to be identified and addressed to reduce your suffering. A support group or therapist can often provide a valuable and safe space to process secondary losses.

Honor Your Losses

There are a lot of different ways you can honor the losses you have experienced. After the death of someone close to you, find ways, big or small, to remember them. Give a donation to their favorite charity or plant a memorial garden in their honor. You could make a memory book or box of special photos, create a playlist of your loved one's favorite songs, eat their favorite candy, or wear a piece of their jewelry. You can also mark the anniversary of their death, birthday, or other significant dates with a unique tradition, like recreating their signature recipe or visiting one of their favorite places.

If you didn't get a say in planning your loved one's final arrangements, or if you had an issue with how a person was memorialized (hello, complex family dynamics surfacing during stressful life events!), you can create your own private memorial ceremony or ritual that feels meaningful to you. Many people talk or write letters to their deceased friends and family members too. That is a normal and healthy way to find an ongoing connection with a person who died.

Manage Collective Grief

It's common to feel stuck or numb in reaction to a mass tragedy, but there are steps you can take to cope. To begin, let yourself feel and sit with your emotions—reminding yourself that whatever you are feeling is valid. Next, resist the urge to doom scroll or overwhelm yourself with horrifying images on the news or social media. Get the information you need to stay informed from a few sources you trust.

To reduce any sense of hopelessness you might be experiencing, engage in activism or advocacy. Donate to a worthy cause if you have the funds, call or write your local representative, or volunteer your time. If those tasks feel overwhelming, focus on caring for yourself and your loved ones. When life becomes too much, it's okay to shrink your world down to a manageable size. Drink water, walk around the block, and breathe. Somedays, that will be all you can do and that is enough.

Finally, bring a little good to this world to combat feelings of cynicism that might be sneaking into your psyche. This could involve doing a random act of kindness for a stranger or expressing your gratitude to a friend or relative. Last year the kids in my neighborhood had a lemonade stand to raise funds to prevent gun violence. If everyone does a little, it can add up to a lot.

Mending a Broken Heart

Everyone, at some point, will have to contend with rejection and heartbreak. As I mentioned, being in love is like being high on cocaine, so when you experience a breakup, it's similar to going through withdrawal. You experience intense wanting and craving for the other person because you can't get your romantic "fix" from them anymore. You struggle to accept the other person's explanations about why they no longer want to be with you. You obsess about what you could have done differently and overanalyze every moment leading up to the end. This is not to mention that you lose part of your identity during a breakup, as your daily routine, social calendar, and even friendships may change. And no explanation will ever be satisfying enough to take away the pain.

I get it. Healing from heartbreak is difficult. It takes tremendous strength to avoid obsessing about your ex. It's common to idealize them and only reflect on the good parts of the relationship. However, you only feed your addiction every time you text your ex, stalk them on social media, replay old messages, or look at their picture. Instead, try listing all the things you dislike about them. When you start to wax poetic about the good times, remind yourself about all the shitty moments. Think about how they load the dishwasher like a psychopath. Reflect on that time when they drank too much during last year's Super Bowl party and were a total dick to your friends. Stop standing in the way of your healing. Burn some sage and get rid of that bad energy, friend.

My friend Bill was instrumental in helping me get over someone I dated in my 20s. I was utterly smitten with this relationship because the guy was several years older and seemed sophisticated and together. When he broke things off with me, I was in a funk. Bill said, "Liz, don't worry about Aarp." I was baffled and asked Bill who "Aarp" was. He said, "You know, AARP, the American Association of Retired Persons." I started laughing hysterically until I almost peed my pants. Having Bill point out the significant age difference made me realize that I was romanticizing my ex and seeing this relationship through rose-colored glasses.

Heartbreak also isn't limited to just romantic relationships. You can experience heartbreak when you check the Find My Friends app on your phone and discover that your college friends are in town but didn't reach out. Or when your best friend uncovers a different part of their identity and now hangs with a new crowd without you. Heartbreak can happen after the loss of any cherished relationship.

How to Help Someone Grieving

Since grief, in all its forms, can be uncomfortable in a culture that glorifies "good vibes only," it can be hard to know what to do if someone close to you experiences a loss. But being a good friend to someone grieving is easier than you think, especially if you embrace the awkwardness. Here are some things you should (and shouldn't do) to be helpful:

DO: Validate your friend's emotions and feelings.
As I mentioned before, the emotions of grief can feel like a roller coaster. Give your friend space to feel whatever they are feeling. That might look like simply reflecting back and paraphrasing what you hear them say, as well as validating their emotions ("This is really hard" or "It makes sense that you feel angry right now").

DO: Give yourself permission to feel awkward or uncomfortable.
It is totally okay if you do not know what to say to someone who has experienced a devastating loss. Let your friend know that you don't know what to say, but also make it clear that you love them and want to support them. If you are unsure how to support your friend, it's fine to ask, "How can I best support you right now?"

DO: Give your friend opportunities to talk about the person who died.
It's common to feel nervous about bringing up the deceased because you're worried that it will bring up overwhelming feelings of sadness. However, your friend may want to talk about the person who died. (And if they don't want to, they'll tell you.) They might even be concerned that their loved one will be forgotten if they don't talk about them or share memories. Give them this opportunity. If you didn't know the person who died, you might also want to ask your friend what this person was like.

DO: Remember important dates.
Specific dates can activate intense grief, such as death dates, court dates associated with divorce or custody hearings, birthdays, holidays, or anniversaries. My client's serious girlfriend broke up with him last year on March 14, also known as Pi Day (the annual recognition of the

mathematical symbol pi for all you awesome math nerds out there). He is a fantastic baker, and he had baked her an apple pie, complete with a lattice top that would impress Julia Child, to commemorate Pi Day.

When March 14 came around again this year, he noticed feelings of sadness, low energy, and distraction resurfacing. We brainstormed some strategies to cope with the anniversary of this challenging breakup, such as getting a massage and taking care not to overload his work schedule on that day. He and I also decided to now refer to this date as "sad pie day," which we agreed would make a stellar band name.

Talk to your friend and see if there are any tough dates coming up for them. They might need your support or company. In addition, don't forget to check in as time goes on. Bereaved individuals typically anticipate that the first year after the death of a loved one will be challenging. It's a year filled with "firsts"—of first special days and events without that person. I often find that people are surprised by how intense the second year of grief can feel when the reality sets in that the loss is permanent.

DO: Make yourself available to hang out or help with tasks.
After a loss, simple tasks can feel really overwhelming. Ask your friend if they would like company for a dreaded errand. For many, even going to the grocery store can feel daunting. They fear running into acquaintances, getting "looks" from people who may know of their loss, or even seeing items they used to buy for a loved one. Helping your friend buy bulk toilet paper at Costco, get their car's oil changed, or handle complex paperwork can be a tremendous support.

DO: Ask their permission before giving suggestions or advice.
When you've experienced grief in the past, you may have found that certain strategies, like joining a support group, taking an exercise class, or meditating, were a massive help. But just because a strategy was a critical part of your healing doesn't mean it will necessarily work for someone else. If you want to share advice or suggestions with a friend,

ask permission first: "Hey, do you mind if I share something that I found helpful in the past?" or "Do you want to talk through some ideas to cope with what you are going through?" This gives your friend a chance to say no if they aren't currently open to feedback or ready to make changes.

DON'T: Exclude them from events and social outings.
You might assume that a grieving friend isn't up for a movie or concert date, but a night out could be just the thing they need to get a welcome break from grief. Keep inviting your grieving friend to events, but provide them with the option to say no if they don't have the emotional capacity or energy to attend.

DON'T: Feel responsible for cheering them up.
Your job is not to remove the pain of your friend's loss. Avoid making comments like "At least you got severance pay" or "At least the breakup happened before the holidays." There is no silver lining in loss, especially when the loss was recent. Asking your friend to look on the bright side sends the message that they shouldn't feel bad or that you are uncomfortable with them in their pain. You truly don't have to fix their pain. Simply being willing to sit with them in their grief is an incredible kindness.

DON'T: Help them down their sorrows.
It might be tempting to soothe a friend's pain from a difficult breakup with a big, boozy night out. However, alcohol will only intensify feelings like sadness and anxiety in the long run. Instead, encourage your friend to engage in healthy coping behaviors by inviting them on a walk, taking a yoga class, or doing something creative together.

DON'T: Make assumptions about their faith traditions or spiritual beliefs.
Your faith may be a profound source of comfort and hope. However, a significant loss can shake someone's spiritual and religious beliefs to the

core, especially if the loss was traumatic or unexpected. Be thoughtful about referencing a specific faith tradition or a particular view of the afterlife in the wake of someone's loss, especially if you don't have a solid understanding of your friend's spiritual or religious beliefs.

DON'T: Bring up your own losses and grief history.
All of us have dealt with, or will deal with, grief in our lives. When someone close to you experiences a loss, it can be tempting to bring up your own grief history as a way to connect. But everyone's losses and experiences are unique. When you bring up your own experience with loss, it takes the focus off of the griever.

The Transformative Nature of Grief

I was 42 years old when I put together the proposal for the book you are now reading. My dad died from cancer when he was 42 years old. When I turned the same age as my dad when he died, something clicked for me. I realized that life is not a drill or a dress rehearsal. It was time to stop talking about writing and actually start writing. I had to take action.

I wouldn't wish the death of a parent on anyone, even though it's something we will all experience at some point, but I also wouldn't change how my grief impacted me. It made me who I am today. Grief helped me clarify my values. Having a sense of my mortality at a young age made me realize that I can't waste time living for someone else. I can't put off what's important until tomorrow because tomorrow isn't guaranteed.

Grief is transformative. A loss or traumatic event changes how you see yourself, others, and the world. You are not the same person after a loss as you were before. Grief is not easy, but it can be powerful. In his book *Finding Meaning: The Sixth Stage of Grief*, David Kessler explains that every loss has meaning. At first, the idea of finding meaning in your loss might make you want to throw this book in the trash. After all, how could anything meaningful possibly come from a gut-wrenching loss? But as Kessler explains, the meaning is not found in the horrible or devastating event itself. Rather, it is found within you and how you learn and grow.

Finding meaning is not about glossing over the pain and sweeping your sorrow under the rug. Healing takes time. So often, individuals who have experienced loss will try to quickly bypass their pain by finding a purpose to cling to, but they first have to accept their new reality. Acceptance is not the same thing as liking your new reality. It's about coming to terms with how things are, as opposed to how you wish they were. Finding meaning also does not mean that your grief has gone away. As writer and grief expert Nora McInerny explains, people don't *move on* from grief. Instead, they *move forward with* their grief.[18]

One remarkable thing about grief is that it has a way of cutting through all the bullshit. After my dad died, I really didn't care as much about what other people thought of me, and I wanted to make darn sure that I wasn't wasting my life. That's not to say that I had it immediately all figured out after my dad's death. I still had a lot to learn, but I did gain some clarity. I stopped sweating the small stuff so much. I had the courage to take on challenges because I knew I could tolerate tough emotions.

Grief doesn't get smaller over time. Instead, you grow around your grief.[19] This speaks to the concept of posttraumatic growth, which refers to the positive psychological change that can occur following adversity. People can grow and change in remarkable ways following difficult circumstances. They may find new sources of meaning and connection that they otherwise wouldn't have. When you experience posttraumatic growth, you may:

- Be open to new opportunities
- Have stronger relationships with others

- Gain a greater appreciation for life

- Develop new perspectives on faith and spirituality

- Have increased confidence in your abilities to overcome challenges

I want to be clear about this point: The losses you have experienced and the challenges you have faced were not the universe or some higher power telling you that you "needed" a lesson. You didn't deserve this. Shitty things sometimes happen in life, and it's not fair. If you have faced a devastating loss and the idea of posttraumatic growth feels foreign or impossible, that's okay. There is nothing wrong with you, and you do not lack resilience. Changes may or may not come later as your pain shifts over time.

I have a former colleague who experienced the death of his child from a genetic disease. In response, he and his wife created an organization that supports caregivers who are going through similar situations. Nothing will ever take away the pain of his loss, but he is creating meaning by easing the suffering of others. By forming connections with other parents, he and his wife are not alone in their grief. The organization honors the love they have for their child and continues the bond that they had with him.

I think of someone grieving a loss like a precious glass vase that shatters and breaks. The vase can't be put together again like it was before the loss. However, the remaining shards of glass can be turned into something beautiful, like a mosaic or stained-glass window. How can you honor your losses in a way that lets you live your life going forward?

Action Items

1. Reflect on your life. What losses, big or small, are you dealing with right now? How have these losses impacted your life or your perspective on life?

2. Grief involves a wide range of emotions. If you are currently experiencing a loss, what are five emotions you are feeling right now?

3. How can you honor or remember the important people in your life who have died?

CHAPTER 8

MAKE IT MEANINGFUL

 He who has a *why* to live for can bear with almost any *how*.

—Friedrich Nietzsche

Happiness versus Meaning

We live in a society that focuses on feeling good. Our culture sends the message that if we aren't happy and feeling good, something is wrong with us. I'm not sure who needs to hear this, but *no one* feels happy all the time. Happiness is fleeting. It comes and goes.

In fact, it's really important to learn how to sit with discomfort without trying to change or fix those feelings because the things we do to feel satisfied in the present often make us feel worse in the long run. Suppose I feel frustrated with work and need to get rid of these uncomfortable feelings as quickly as possible to feel happy again. In that case, I might buy a dress I don't need on Amazon or shove a cupcake in my face. Other people might say "fuck it" and take a bunch of tequila shots with their friends or meet up with an ex to get that quick feel-good fix. But these things don't make you happier in the long term. It's more likely that these actions will lead to guilt or even a shame spiral.

It's for this reason that I encourage my clients to seek meaning rather than happiness. Without meaning, we feel empty inside. As psychologist Dr. Scott Barry Kaufman writes, "It seems that happiness has more to do with having your needs satisfied, getting what you want, and feeling good, whereas meaning is more related to uniquely human activities such as developing a personal identity, expressing the self, and consciously integrating one's past, present, and future experiences."[20]

The great thing about making meaning is that you can participate in actions that create meaning independent from your current mood. For example, I greatly value connection, so I love sending my friends and family postcards. I constantly hunt for witty, funny, inappropriate, empowering, and inspirational stationery. I may not remember my friends' birthdays, but I will send them a silly postcard on a random Tuesday in February. This activity creates a lot of meaning in my life. Even on my lowest days, I can always find a connection by making someone smile when they open their mailbox.

When you invest in meaningful activities, it often lends itself to feeling good in the future, even if you have negative feelings at the moment. Being a writer and being creative is part of my identity. That said, some days I would rather not open my computer. I might feel stuck or concerned that I have nothing valuable to say. I procrastinate by doing laundry, unloading the dishwasher, or reorganizing my shoes. But I never regret a writing session.

The Four Pillars of Meaning

Researcher and author Emily Esfahani Smith identified four pillars of meaning in her TED Talk "There's More to Life Than Being Happy."[21] She notes that despite the many improvements in our overall quality of life over the past several decades, the suicide rate in the United States has continued to increase over the past 30 years. Even though there are more ways than ever before to feel momentarily happy, many people still feel hopeless, depressed, and lonely. To increase meaning in our lives, Esfahani Smith suggests focusing on the four core elements of meaning: belonging, purpose, transcendence, and storytelling.

Belonging

Individuals who feel connected to their friends, family, and community tend to believe that their lives are more meaningful. Having this sense of belonging is different from simply "fitting in." Belonging is not about being accepted simply because you like the same sports team, wear the right clothes, or practice the same religion as someone else. True belonging is rooted in love and allows you to be valued for who you are. As Brené Brown explains, "Fitting in is about assessing a situation and becoming who you need to be to be accepted. Belonging, on the other hand, doesn't require us to *change* who we are; it requires us to *be* who we are."[22]

Purpose

People also gain meaning by finding a sense of purpose in their lives. Purpose is about finding your sense of "why"—that which drives you to get out of bed every day. This is not the same thing as pressuring yourself to find your "passion" (i.e., a job or hobby at which you excel) and expecting that everything will fall into place. (PSA: People rarely "find" their passion. Most people develop it over time with persistence and grit.) Purpose is about discovering how you can be helpful in the world and using your strengths in a way that makes your life feel worthwhile.

Transcendence

Transcendence is a mental state of engagement and intense focus, also known by some psychologists as "flow." You may refer to this state as being "in the zone." Some people find their flow in creative pursuits like drawing, knitting, or painting. Others find it by playing sports, writing, being in nature, or gardening. When you are in a flow state, you become absorbed in the moment and lose track of time. Similar to the concept of mindfulness, you are not judging yourself or thinking about the past or future. Transcendence also occurs when you feel a sense of awe about the world and your place in it.

Storytelling

Storytelling is the process of reflecting on your life and crafting a meaningful narrative from your lived experience. The words you use and the stories you tell yourself are powerful. For example, if you have struggled to find satisfying employment, do you define yourself as a failure or as someone who has persistence? If you are looking for a romantic partner, do you view yourself as unlovable or as someone who has the patience to wait for the right person? How can you tell the story of your life in a manner that feels empowering and meaningful? Reality is a social construct, and there is no one absolute truth. There are multiple ways to interpret experiences and events. How can you tell your story and interpret your experiences in a manner that feels empowering? If you were a filmmaker working on an inspirational story about your life, what events and themes would you include?

Identifying Your Values

After the birth of my oldest child, like most parents, I was running on fumes. The sleep deprivation of having a tiny human hit me hard. I felt, and probably looked, like a hot mess. I had no idea how I would return to my career or feel like myself again. One of the ways I managed to refill my internal gas tank during that time was through 10-to-20-minute guided meditations. The meditation would always begin by asking me to identify my purpose and what gives my life meaning. That's a broad and abstract question, but I repeatedly heard my inner voice saying, *I am authentic, creative, intentional, and useful.* I didn't know it at the time, but I was clarifying my values. Looking back over the past few years, I see how identifying those values influenced my priorities and decisions.

As the old saying goes, "If you don't stand for something, you'll fall for anything." I couldn't agree more. Taking the time to identify your core values gives your life direction. It's like having a compass so you know which way to go. Time will pass no matter what, so it's up to you to use that time in a meaningful way by having goals to work toward. When I talk about having goals, I don't mean exhausting yourself by hustling for the next big thing. I am talking about intentionally living your life in alignment with your values. Unlike a rigid five-year plan, values give you flexibility in expressing your priorities.

This flexibility is key in a world that is incredibly overwhelming. There are many choices about what to wear, watch on TV, study, and read. You have to make countless decisions about with whom to spend your time, what to look at online, what hobbies or passions to pursue, and how to make a living. When my grandmother was my age, there were two types of cereal to decide between at the grocery store. Now when I go to the grocery store, I'm faced with 4,000 different types of cereal. To pick a breakfast food for my kids, I have to decide which brand tastes good, isn't a total sugar bomb, doesn't have red dye 40, and has some protein and fiber. Gah! And that's just the cereal aisle.

Decision-making can feel burdensome in these situations because of a phenomenon known as the paradox of choice, which reflects our tendency to have a difficult time choosing when there are several things to choose from. And the more options we have, the less satisfied we are with our final choice. We second-guess ourselves and ruminate on the choices we didn't make. This leads to decision fatigue. It's exhausting having to constantly decide what gets our precious time, energy, attention, and money. When we make choices stemming from our values, we can better manage the paradox of choice in the modern world.

While conducting fieldwork in graduate school, I had the great fortune to be paired with Judson Richardson, whom I now consider both a cherished friend and a trusted colleague. He introduced me to an activity called the value sort, which helps you reflect on what you prioritize most in life. We would cut out different value words on paper and mix them up on the table. Then we would have clients sort through the words and identify which spoke to them. It was a powerful exercise and one that I now regularly use.

The value sort is an activity you can do yourself. If you are feeling inspired and have a few dollars to burn, there are value card decks you can buy online. You can also use the list on the next page. The first step is to go through the list and circle any values that speak to you. After you have completed that step, go through and pick your top ten values, then your top five values. Next, rank your five values in order of importance. What core values get the top two spots? These are the values that can best guide your actions and decisions.

If you don't see a value listed, feel free to add your own. You can also repeat this exercise anytime you feel the need to connect to yourself. I try to do this activity at least once annually. Your values and priorities can change over time, and that's perfectly okay.

Get Smart with Your Goals

After you have identified your top core values, then the real fun can begin. It's more than just painting these words on a board, like some of the wall art you might see at HomeGoods. (Nothing like a piece of reclaimed wood instructing you to "Live, Laugh, Love" when your kid woke you up six times last night, but I digress.) You've got to turn those values into action. Otherwise, they'll remain abstract concepts with no real impact on your life. Turning your values into action allows you to live with intention rather than let the momentum of the daily grind take over.

As I mentioned earlier, authenticity is one of my core values. Being authentic is essential to me because the more comfortable I am in

List of Values

Abundance	Creativity	Integrity	Safety
Acceptance	Curiosity	Intelligence	Security
Accomplishment	Dedication	Intentionality	Self-actualization
Accountability	Dignity	Intuition	Self-discipline
Accuracy	Diversity	Job security	Self-expression
Achievement	Drive	Joy	Self-reliance
Adaptability	Efficiency	Justice	Self-respect
Adventure	Environment	Kindness	Serenity
Advocacy	Equality	Knowledge	Service
Affection	Ethics	Leadership	Simplicity
Alertness	Excellence	Learning	Spirituality
Altruism	Excitement	Legacy	Sportsmanship
Ambition	Fairness	Leisure	Stability
Attentiveness	Faith	Love	Status
Authenticity	Family	Loyalty	Stewardship
Awareness	Fearlessness	Mastery	Structure
Balance	Financial stability	Nature	Success
Beauty	Fitness	Openness	Teamwork
Belonging	Forgiveness	Optimism	Thrift
Boldness	Freedom	Order	Time
Brilliance	Friendship	Originality	Timeliness
Career	Fun	Parenting	Tolerance
Caring	Generosity	Passion	Tradition
Challenge	Giving back	Patience	Transparency
Charity	Grace	Patriotism	Travel
Cleanliness	Gratitude	Peace	Trust
Collaboration	Growth	Perseverance	Truth
Comfort	Harmony	Personal	Understanding
Commitment	Health	fulfillment	Uniqueness
Community	Home	Playfulness	Unity
Compassion	Honesty	Power	Usefulness
Competence	Hope	Pride	Vision
Competition	Humility	Productivity	Vulnerability
Confidence	Humor	Recognition	Wealth
Connection	Impact	Reliability	Well-being
Contentment	Inclusion	Resourcefulness	Wisdom
Contribution	Independence	Respect	Wonder
Cooperation	Individuality	Responsibility	
Courage	Initiative	Restraint	
Courtesy	Innovation	Risk-taking	

my skin, the better I can serve my clients as a therapist. Authenticity allows me to connect and be fully present with my clients. After I had kids, I gave some thought to how I could translate authenticity into action. One of the ways I decided to practice authenticity was to improve boundaries around my time. I looked hard at my schedule and determined how many client sessions I could realistically include. I stopped taking client sessions in the evenings since I have never been, nor will I ever be, a night person. I started saying no to consulting work and volunteer obligations that I didn't have the capacity for. In my personal life, I became more intentional about the relationships I invested in and the information I consumed. I started practicing self-compassion and self-acceptance. All of these steps helped me feel less stressed so I had more energy to be myself.

There are no right or wrong ways to turn your values into action. You don't have to go all *Eat, Pray, Love* and make grandiose changes to your life unless you want to. If you're going to travel to India and live in an ashram like Elizabeth Gilbert, that rocks. But only some people have the resources and flexibility to do that, and it's not a requirement for a meaningful life. Instead, you can bring your core values to your everyday life in big and small ways. Brené Brown explains, "I don't have to chase extraordinary moments to find happiness—it's right in front of me if I'm paying attention and practicing gratitude."[23]

Start by asking yourself some questions. It's time to dig deep and start visualizing what your life could be if you lived by your values:

- What do you want more of in your life?

- What do you want less of in your life?

- What is one small step you could take to get more of what you want in your life?

- How can you bring your core values into your work and personal life?

- What might get in the way of turning your core values into action?

- How can you exercise your values today, this week, and this month?

Once you have done some reflection, it's time to identify goals. Sometimes the word *goal* can be intimidating. It conjures up memories of performance reviews, strict diets, and failed New Year's resolutions. Reframe what goals mean for you so they feel more manageable. One way to do so is to make them SMART goals—meaning they are specific, measurable, achievable, realistic, and time bound. If a goal is too lofty or vague, it will be challenging to know where to start.

Let's say you have a core value of connection. A nonspecific goal for this value might be to "Meet new people" or "Appreciate my relationships." There is nothing wrong with those statements, but you're more likely to succeed if your goals are more precise. Here are a few ways to make these goals smarter:

TODAY: Send a text to my college friend to say hello and let him know that I am thinking about him.

THIS WEEK: Buy a card and stamps. Send a note to my aunt.

THIS MONTH: Invite an acquaintance to coffee.

THIS YEAR: Join a community organization or club.

Your goals can be short term or long term, simple or complex. Either way, your goals should be about what you want in life instead of what you don't want. You don't want your goals to feel like punishment or strict rules and regulations. For example, rather than saying, "Stop dating unavailable people," you might aspire to avoid alcohol on first dates to better assess the person's character.

Tune In to Your Intuition

If you're having trouble identifying concrete goals for yourself, don't panic. Figuring out what you want is easier said than done in today's hectic world. This is where mindfulness comes in. The great thing about mindfulness is that it's more than just a strategy to regulate and calm your nervous system. It's a tool that allows you to slow down and tap into your intuition, that calm and confident sense of knowing. You can think of your intuition as that quiet feeling of truth and clarity within yourself. Your intuition is the opposite of your judgmental inner critic; it's the voice of your wisest self speaking.

Do you know why people often get the best ideas in the shower? That's because it's a place where they can allow their minds to wander freely without the distraction of their phones, televisions, computers, and all the other noise of the outside world. It's a place where they can tune in to their innermost self.

I tend to do my best thinking when I am on a walk. It allows me to take a break from the roles that I perform during the day—therapist, spouse, parent, and friend—and gives me the space to think in more creative ways. Listening to my favorite tunes on the local trails boosts my mood, energy, and confidence. On days I am dragging, I will borrow some of Lizzo, Harry Styles, and Beyoncé's swagger to help my ideas flow. I will often even stop in the middle of a walk to write down new insights that have come to me.

Therefore, if you need some help identifying values-based goals, see what your intuition has to say. There are several ways to tap into your intuition:

- Meditate, do some yoga, spend time in a quiet place like a library or an art museum, or engage in any other activity that brings about a sense of calm and focus.

- Let yourself be creative by drawing, painting, crafting, cooking, sketching, or doodling. Engaging your brain in nonverbal activities can help you express yourself and bring about new perspectives.

- Use your five senses to reconnect to your surroundings and the present moment. This gives your brain a break from thinking about the past or future so that you can better listen to your inner wisdom. You can even use the 5-4-3-2-1 grounding exercise from chapter 3 to name five things you see, four things you feel, three things you hear, two things you smell, and one thing you taste.

- Reflect on a previous event that happened and ask yourself if you had a gut feeling that you ignored at the time. One of my clients recently told me about a situation when she was unsure if she should say yes to being a bridesmaid in a childhood friend's wedding. Her gut told her to decline because she was uncertain if she felt close to, or even liked, this person anymore, but her people-pleasing side took over. She agreed to join the wedding party despite her initial reservations. As time passed and she realized the extent of the wedding party obligations (a five-day bachelorette party in Hawaii, a champagne bridal shower at the Ritz, and never-ending group texts), she realized that being a bridesmaid was an enormous financial and emotional mistake. She backed out to avoid putting herself into debt and spending considerable time and energy on someone she didn't like all that much. This experience taught her the importance of listening to her intuition.

- Get a change of scenery or mix up your routine. Being in a new environment can bring about insight and reflection. I love riding on the metro or bus, visiting new neighborhoods and cities, and seeing how the novelty of a new place sparks creativity and insight.

- Escape to nature. Being in the natural world brings about a sense of awe and gives you a chance to disconnect from mental chatter and technology.

- Do a mundane physical activity like walking or running, chopping veggies, weeding the garden, or sweeping your house. The repetitive movements can feel soothing and allow you to access your intuitive mind.

Consider intuition a practice that develops over time. Another benefit to developing your intuition is that it helps you feel closer to people. There is nothing better than the feeling I get from an uncanny coincidence, like when I email someone only to find that they were about to text me. Or when I realize that I am reading the same book or thinking about the same idea as a client. Tapping into my intuition gives me a sense that we are all connected somehow.

Got Some Change?

Change can be difficult even when you set goals that are in alignment with your core values. Remember how your brain loves the familiar? That's why sustaining new behaviors is tough, even when you know the behaviors are good for you and consistent with what you desire. You might take three steps forward and two (or fifteen) steps back, making it seem like you're not making any progress. But change isn't necessarily linear. Rather, change is a cyclical process that happens in stages, so you will sometimes take unexpected detours, move in reverse, or even go in circles.

When thinking about change, it can be helpful to understand the transtheoretical model of change, which was developed by James Prochaska, John Norcross, and Carlo DiClemente and outlined in their book *Changing for Good*. In their book, they describe the following stages of change that people move through. I see myself regularly cycling through these stages of change when it comes to getting consistent physical activity. Sometimes I am on top of it when it comes to fitting movement and stretching into my schedule and other times not so much.

Precontemplation

Precontemplation is the stage where you lack awareness that something needs to change. You don't plan on adjusting your behavior. An example of this would be someone who smokes cigarettes and doesn't intend to quit. A person in this stage typically has not yet experienced any severe negative consequences or may be in denial about their behavior.

I was in the precontemplation stage regarding physical activity during college and my early 20s. I would occasionally go to the gym with a friend or roommate or after a particularly boozy New Year's resolution ("OMG, you guys, this is going to be *the* year that I get in the best shape of my life! I swear!"), but most of the time, I didn't think about the importance of exercise. I didn't understand back then the vital role physical activity plays in maintaining good mental health (though I wish I had!).

Contemplation

Contemplation is the stage of change when you know something in your life is off, but you're still ambivalent about taking any action. I find myself in this stage often. I know I could benefit from more movement, but I am unsure how best to fit it into my routine. Often, during contemplation, my ever-present inner critic, Nelson, chimes in:

NELSON: You do not have time to exercise. You are on a book deadline. You only have time to write, write, write!

LIZ: I'm sure that's precisely why I need to exercise, Nelson. Physical activity helps manage stress and anxiety.

NELSON: Yeah, but you might die soon. And who would finish your book then?

LIZ: Geez, Nelson! I know everyone will die someday, but the odds are good that I am not kicking the bucket tomorrow. I think I can take 20 minutes to go on a walk or bike ride. Also, exercise is good for longevity. That's called science.

NELSON: Tell yourself whatever you need to hear, slacker. You don't have time to exercise. Get back to your computer.

LIZ: Stop calling me a slacker, asshat.

(Cut to me getting up from my computer occasionally to stretch or walk outside.)

Preparation

Preparation occurs when you decide to take action and experiment with small steps that move you in the direction of change. You might educate yourself on the steps needed to change your behavior, make a specific plan, visualize your life after the change is complete, and buy anything you need to make the change happen.

When I am in the preparation stage, I schedule physical activity on my calendar and research different workouts. I leave my workout gear out so that I have to practically trip over it on my way to do laundry. I contemplate whether I should try Pilates, cross-training, barre workouts, dancing, or running. I've also been known to buy cute workout gear during this stage. I convince myself that floral leggings and new sneakers will make me a dedicated fitness buff. (This hasn't worked so far, but I will probably keep trying. I'm currently wearing yoga pants with no intention of doing yoga today.)

Action

The action stage is self-explanatory. This stage of change is when you start doing the work. I haul my ass out of bed early to go on a walk or take a cycling class. And I inevitably feel so freaking amazing after a few workouts. Part of me says, *This is so easy! I can keep these workouts up indefinitely. I love my new lifestyle.*

Maintenance

The maintenance phase describes your efforts to keep up with the new behavior for the long haul. And this is where the trouble comes in for me, folks. I do well keeping up my new workout routine for a while, but then something inevitably happens, like my kid getting struck with the stomach flu. Even though I use radical acceptance to deal with the aftermath of cleaning up what resembles a scene from *The Exorcist*, when I've been up most of the night tending to a puking kid, it means that the likelihood of me working out that next day is zilch, zero, nada. And that's okay—because life happens. Maintenance occurs when I get back on track with physical activity later in the week.

Relapse

The real challenge comes when my second kid gets sick, I have a big work assignment due, and now I have missed an entire week of workouts. At this point in the stages of change, I officially relapse. I slip into my old behavior patterns, preferring to sleep in or watch the local news rather than get my sweat on. This doesn't mean that I have failed or undone my previous progress. It's a natural part of the stages of change.

When I find myself slipping into old patterns, I use this as an opportunity for growth. I practice self-compassion by recognizing the futility of trying to do (and be good at) all the things all at once. I also check in with what will work and what won't work. For example, long workouts may not always be practical at this stage of my life. With that information, I work to overcome the relapse by sneaking in short bursts of physical activity throughout the day, like stretching or walking between client sessions and doing push-ups against the counter while my coffee brews. Life isn't so much about being able to juggle all the balls in the air at once. It's about picking them back up again when you drop one. I can always begin again.

Termination

Termination occurs when you feel confident in maintaining your new behavior over the long run. You've established healthier habits and can keep them going without much effort or vigilance. The temptation to slip into old behavior patterns is gone, and you gain a new self-image. I have never reached this stage of being able to effortlessly incorporate physical activity into my life. If you have, please let me know what it's like to feel like Serena Williams.

On the other hand, I have reached the termination stage regarding my relationship with alcohol. When I initially toyed with the idea of going alcohol-free, I spent time in the preparation stage by immersing myself in books about sobriety (a.k.a. the genre of "quit lit"). I spent over a year toggling between being alcohol-free and attempting moderation. I finally picked a date and stopped drinking booze altogether. At this point, I rarely feel any cravings or temptations and view myself as a nondrinker. Will I ever drink again? It's unlikely. I am done cycling through the stages of change.

Action Items

1. Using the values list provided in the chapter, determine your top two core values.

2. Identify two SMART goals that put these two core values into action. Make sure to identify actions you can take today, this week, this month, and this year.

3. Consider how you might use the stages of change model to create a new healthy habit. Where are you in the process of change?

CHAPTER 9

YOUR MENTAL HEALTH FOR THE LONG HAUL

 You can't go back and make a new start, but you can start right now and make a brand new ending.

—James R. Sherman

Looking for More?

Even though there are a lot of strategies you can use to improve your mental health on your own, you may decide to take that plunge and pursue therapy. Perhaps you're at a point in life where you feel like you can't go it alone anymore. There is no shame in needing additional care. If you had cancer or heart disease, you wouldn't be expected to figure out how to heal yourself. Mental health conditions are no different. Therapy is likely necessary if you are:

- Having trouble managing the activities of daily life

- Feeling stuck

- Struggling in your relationships

- Experiencing thoughts of self-harm or suicide

- Being told by trusted friends or family to consider mental health treatment

Finding a therapist can be challenging in this day and age, where there is a high demand for services and long waiting lists. But knowing where to look, what to look for, and what questions to ask can make the process easier. One of the greatest places to start is to ask around your social network. If you have a friend in the mental health field, ask if they can give you some referrals for clinicians or practices that might be a good fit for you. You can also ask your primary care doctor or OB-GYN for names. I often find that local community groups on social media can be a source of resources as well. But make sure you do your own work to research the referrals you get from your friends or community.

If your connections can't provide you with referrals, there are online directories of licensed therapists where you can search by zip code, specialty, education, experience, and more. Psychology Today and therapist.com are two good places to start. You may also feel more comfortable with a provider of a specific gender, race, cultural background, religion, or sexual orientation. In addition, consider location and accessibility when narrowing your search. Some providers meet in person, while others provide teletherapy.

You will also want to carefully consider a provider's credentials to ensure they are licensed to provide psychotherapy. Qualified mental health professionals must pass licensing exams, stay up to date on continuing education to keep their licenses current, and uphold legal and ethical standards. Individuals who provide wellness, personal, or fitness coaching do not have to abide by the same strict ethical and legal requirements as licensed therapists, so check the experience and qualifications *very* carefully before hiring a "life coach." My friend's ex-boyfriend, who has yet to keep a job for more than two months at a time and sustains himself solely on chocolate protein shakes, is now marketing himself as a life coach. On the other hand, one of my dear friends has her masters in positive psychology and is an absolutely fabulous life coach. Buyer beware!

Qualified providers of therapy typically have these credentials:

- Psychologist (PsyD or PhD)

- Psychiatrist (MD or DO)*

- Licensed clinical social worker (LICSW or LCSW)

- Licensed marriage and family therapist (LMFT)

- Licensed professional counselor (LPC)

- Licensed clinical alcohol and drug abuse counselor (LCADAC)

How to Find a Therapist That Doesn't Suck

The most crucial factor that determines whether or not therapy will be successful is the fit between you and your therapist. You need to feel good about the relationship you have with them. You need to trust that they have your best interests at heart and feel like they respect you, no matter what you are going through. You won't be able to talk about difficult experiences or challenging emotions if you don't feel safe opening up to them.

All therapists have different styles and personalities. For example, I tend to provide my clients with suggestions, validation, feedback, and psychoeducation. I also like to swear, break into song, use jazz hands, and help my clients find a funny name for their inner critic. Other therapists tend to listen, reflect, and guide clients to find their own answers. Still others light aromatherapy candles, have 97 choices of herbal tea, and wear colorful crocheted shawls. You've got to find the right vibe for you. I recognize that I will not be the right therapist for everyone. If someone meets with me and later decides that they want to pursue services with someone else, that is perfectly okay! My goal is for

---

* While some psychiatrists do provide therapy, most mainly prescribe and manage medication for mental health conditions.

clients to have the best possible therapeutic experience, whether with me or another provider.

When looking for a therapist, you will want to ask questions to determine if this person is a good fit for you. It's absolutely okay to interview your therapist either via email or in an initial call with them prior to scheduling your first session. You want to get a sense of your comfort level interacting with them. You can ask a potential therapist questions like these:

- What sort of training, education, and experience do you have?

- What does a typical session look like? What can I expect?

- Do you specialize in any particular issue or problem?

- What type of therapy do you provide? How do you approach therapy?

- Is your approach to therapy a good match for the issues I want to focus on?

- How will I know when I no longer need to be in therapy?

- Do you conduct sessions via telehealth, in person, or both?

- What is your rate and how do you accept payment? Do you accept insurance?

You should also assess if they have the qualities of a good mental health professional. Not all mental health professionals are created equal, and I want you to have a satisfying experience. A therapist with lots of degrees or a doctorate is not necessarily better than a master's-level practitioner. In your initial interactions and early sessions with a therapist, you should look for someone who:

- Exhibits warmth and compassion

- Is nonjudgmental when discussing your concerns

- Has clear professional boundaries

- Does not try to be your friend or make the session about them

- Is up to speed on research and new developments in the mental health field

- Provides resources, books, and activities for you to reference outside of the sessions

- Upholds your confidentiality

- Checks in regularly about how you feel regarding your progress in therapy

- Remembers essential details about what you have shared in previous sessions

- Is attentive and engaged in your session

- Prioritizes your goals

- Asks thought-provoking questions

A colleague of mine has compared starting therapy to shopping. Generally, within the first 30 days of buying an item, you can decide to keep, exchange, or return it. Therapy is similar. If the first few sessions go well, you can feel good about sticking with your provider. But if a few sessions go by and you feel like your therapist isn't a good match for you, try searching around for someone else.

If you decide that things aren't working out with your current provider, I encourage you to bring your concerns up in a session before switching to another mental health professional. While it might be tempting to ghost them, it's very possible this provider might be a good fit but you two just need to get on the same page. Just like you didn't like getting ghosted by that girl you met last summer at the waterfront, therapists don't like being ghosted either. We would much rather have an opportunity to make adjustments or provide resources. By letting your therapist know what's not working, they can clarify your goals or make therapy more action oriented. If that doesn't bring about desired improvements, then you can work toward finding a new provider.

You may also decide that therapy, in general, isn't suitable for you at this point in your life. That said, therapy can be hard and uncomfortable at times. People often share things in counseling that they have never talked about before. After building trust and rapport, your therapist may also challenge you and serve as a source of accountability for changes you want to make in your life. Make sure you are not ending therapy out of a reluctance to look inward and do the emotional work necessary for growth.

Addressing the (White Lady) Elephant in the Room

Our mental health workforce has a significant diversity problem. If you belong to an underrepresented or marginalized community, it's no surprise that finding a therapist who represents you or speaks your language is extremely difficult, if not damn near impossible. Just take a moment to scroll through most mental health provider directories, and you'll find that it's primarily a bunch of White ladies smiling back at you. As Taylor Swift says in her song "Anti-Hero": "It's me. Hi. I'm the problem, it's me."

In 2019, 70 percent of social workers and 88 percent of mental health counselors were White, while 40 percent of the U.S. population identified with a different racial or ethnic group.[24] Why does this matter? As Jor-El Caraballo, a therapist and author, once told me, "It's normal for clients of color to come into the therapy space skeptical of their providers and their ability to appropriately help. This skepticism is rooted in current and historical practices in health and medicine."[25] A person of color or a member of an underrepresented group often must educate their therapist on their experience and culture. Microaggressions, racism, and economic disparities can be difficult to discuss with someone who has no personal understanding of those issues. In addition, a mental health workforce of primarily White people impacts the subjects that are taught in graduate counseling and psychology programs, the questions on licensure exams, and the mental health topics researched in academia.

As Caraballo went on to explain to me, "White therapists, while well-intentioned, struggle to comprehend the amount of emotional labor Black folks and people of color do in navigating spaces and systems not built with them in mind." Therapists must do academic and real-life research to learn about their clients' cultures and communities in order to provide a safe therapeutic space. If you are a person of color, you should not feel any shame about seeking a culturally humble therapist who will work hard to understand your unique experience. Being culturally humble means that your therapist is committed to ongoing self-reflection and self-critique to gain greater awareness of their inherent bias, privileges, and beliefs. They recognize the power dynamics and imbalances in our society and want to fix those disparities.

The need for more diverse mental health practitioners is gaining awareness, but we have a long way to go. In the meantime, here are a few steps you can take to increase the likelihood that a therapist will be a good fit for you:

- Compile a list of what issues you would like to address in therapy so you can look for therapists with relevant experience in those areas.

- Research therapists on BIPOC-specific directories, like Clinicians of Color, Inclusive Therapists, the Asian Mental Health Collective Directory, Latinx Therapy, Therapy for Black Girls, the Boris Lawrence Henson Foundation, or the Black Mental Health Alliance database.

- Assess the therapist's comfort level in working with racial and ethnic minority groups and other underrepresented populations. Are they comfortable with you asking questions about their experiences working with people of color or marginalized communities? What language or terms do they use to discuss these issues? Does the therapist have photos of people that look like you on their website or social media profile?

- Inquire if the therapist has experience supporting BIPOC clients with the processing and debriefing of high-profile news events.

- Ask how the therapist addresses and incorporates social justice into their work with clients.

Preparing for Your Appointment

The more invested and engaged you are in therapy, the more you will get out of it. That starts with preparing for your first appointment. You might want to jot down a few notes or questions beforehand so you don't forget any pertinent information. Have information about your current prescriptions and health history on hand. Even if your therapist is not a medical professional, they still want to be aware of any medications or health conditions that might impact your mental health.

During the first session, your therapist will ask you why you are seeking therapy. Don't be afraid to answer their questions openly and honestly. Therapists appreciate it when you give a detailed account of when your symptoms started and how those symptoms are interfering with your day-to-day life and goals. You may have seen videos on social media that discuss certain mental health symptoms and recognized yourself in that content. Bring that up to your therapist. I also ask my clients about their alcohol and drug use and how much time they spend on their phones and other forms of technology. It might feel awkward answering those questions openly, but your therapist isn't going to judge you. They are gathering information to create a plan to help you feel better.

I also always ask my clients what their success in therapy would look like. This gives me a better sense of the problem and informs potential goals for our work together. Take a moment and pretend that all of your challenges magically disappeared overnight. When you woke up the following day, what would be different or better about your life? What would your habits and routines look like? What would you do more of or less of?

Give some thought to what you envision for therapy as well. For example, are you seeking long-term treatment that moves at a slower pace? Or do you prefer faster-paced, short-term, solution-focused therapy? Do you want to focus on discussing the past, the present, or both? Finally, consider if you would like to have a therapist who mostly listens and reflects, offers more active thoughts and suggestions, or demonstrates a mix of both styles.

Things to Discuss with Your Therapist (or Ponder Yourself)

If you have never been in therapy, you might be unsure of what to bring up in sessions. Here's the good news: Anything you want to discuss is fair game in therapy. As I mentioned before, your therapist will not judge you or think you are weird. (And if you feel your therapist is judging you, bring that up in session or find someone new.) Here are a few topic areas to help get the conversations rolling:

- Your biggest fears and disappointments

- How your past is impacting you today

- Previous traumatic events you've experienced

- Your goals, hopes, and dreams

- What your family is like

- Losses and transitions you've experienced

- Times you've felt embarrassed or ashamed

- The most important people in your life

- Times when you've felt angry, irritated, or annoyed

- How you spend your time

- Your pet peeves or emotional triggers

- What you believe about yourself, other people, and the world

- How you cope with stress

- The role technology and social media play in your life

- Your patterns of behavior

- What makes you excited, joyful, or curious

- The thoughts in your head

Don't hesitate to bring up something "small" in the session. Often, what you think is insignificant or meaningless might point to a larger pattern or issue. My job as a therapist is to hold up a mirror and reflect back what I hear from you so that you can make connections and gain insight. One of my new clients, Alex, casually said to me, "I've been spending a lot of time on my phone." I explored that comment with her further and discovered that she often was on TikTok at night as a way to distract herself from her stressful job. She would stay up later than intended and then feel tired the next day. This contributed to her difficulties in regulating her emotions and engaging in activities she used to enjoy, like boxing, trivia night, and cooking. Because Alex mentioned her phone usage in the session, we were able to discuss strategies to be more intentional and mindful of technology, like charging her phone in the kitchen at night and putting her phone in "do not disturb" mode.

One casual comment prompted a conversation that triggered a chain reaction of positive change in Alex's life.

Sometimes my clients will ask me if they should do anything to prepare for their therapy sessions. It's really up to you. I have clients show up to sessions and discuss whatever is on their minds. Other clients jot down their thoughts throughout the week and use that to start our conversations. Some will discuss an article or book they read that prompted them to engage in self-reflection or brought up something within them. There is no right or wrong way to "do" therapy, but I encourage you to jot down any insights from your sessions so you can refer to those notes later and see your progress.

How to Afford Therapy if You Are Short on Cash

So what do you do when you want to go to therapy but don't have the financial resources to do so? It may take some effort and persistence, but there are ways to make mental health treatment more affordable. Here are a few to consider.

Talk to Your Therapist about Your Financial Situation

Talk to your therapist if you are facing financial challenges. They might be able to work with you. They can space out your appointments to make treatment more affordable or discuss skills you can practice for homework between sessions to keep your progress going. Your therapist can also provide you with paperwork to seek reimbursement from your insurance company.

Ask Your Therapist if They Offer a Sliding Scale or Pro Bono Appointments

Some therapists also offer a sliding scale or pro bono appointments. A sliding scale means that the therapist's fee is adjusted based on your income. Many therapists also have one or two pro bono (free) spots on their caseload reserved for clients who do not have the resources for therapy.

Check with Your Insurance or Employee Assistance Plan

I know the last thing anyone wants to do is spend precious time on the phone listening to instrumental versions of '80s hits while stuck on hold. But if you have insurance, it's worth giving the company a call or deep diving into your benefits on their website. Mental health benefits are increasingly covered by insurance. Your benefits may include talk therapy, psychiatry, inpatient services, partial hospitalization, substance abuse treatment, and emergency care or crisis intervention. In addition, talk to your human resource department and find out if short-term counseling and other wellness benefits are available through your employee assistance plan.

Check with Local Community Mental Health Organizations

Local nonprofit community health organizations often offer affordable therapy options. They typically receive funding from private donors, grants, and the government to provide services to those in need. Often, your local health or social services department will have these organizations listed on their website. Sometimes there is funding available to address specific issues. I previously worked at a nonprofit that provides low-cost or no-cost therapy to victims of crime and trauma, those impacted by interpersonal and sexual violence, and children affected by grief.

Consider a Therapist in Training

Many colleges, universities, and nonprofit counseling centers offer an option to see a therapist in training at low or no cost. These are typically graduate-level students supervised by a licensed mental health provider. Don't let the lack of experience deter you from trying this. Therapists in training usually are highly motivated and have fewer clients than licensed clinicians, so they can prioritize you. Interns also receive a lot of oversight from licensed clinicians, even more than the average clinician in private practice, and tend to be up to date on the latest interventions, research, and books.

Try Group Therapy

Group therapy focuses on promoting positive change and personal growth, and it is generally less expensive than individual therapy. In group therapy, one or more therapists work with a small group, typically six to twelve participants. Group therapy offers many of the same benefits and can be equally impactful as individual therapy. What's more, it decreases the sense of isolation that mental health struggles can bring and allows you to connect with others going through similar issues. Group therapy also provides an excellent opportunity to practice communicating and relating to others in new ways.

Attend a Support Group

Online or in-person support groups can be beneficial, especially when you're dealing with concerns such as interpersonal violence, addiction, grief, caregiving, or a specific illness. Hearing other people's experiences can make you feel less alone. For example, the Trevor Project has an online network called TrevorSpace, a safe and affirming space for young people in the LGBTQIA+ community. Support groups can also be a great place to share resources and coping strategies. Before joining a support group, you will want to research how the group is run and moderated to ensure this is an emotionally safe space to share. Unlike group therapy, support groups may or may not be run by licensed mental health professionals, as they are often organized by volunteers or peer-support facilitators.

Call a Crisis Prevention Hotline

Many people are aware of suicide prevention hotlines and text support, but there are also crisis prevention hotlines available for other issues. For example, crisis support is available for addiction, gambling, HIV and AIDS, sexual assault, interpersonal and domestic violence, child abuse, and eating disorders. Some hotlines are also specific to specific groups, such as veterans, the LGBTQIA+ community, and teens and young adults. The following hotlines are just some examples available in the U.S.:

- Childhelp National Child Abuse Hotline: 1-800-422-4453

- Crisis Text Line: Text HOME to 741741

- National Domestic Violence Hotline: 1-800-799-7233

- National Sexual Assault Hotline: 1-800-656-4673

- National Suicide and Crisis Lifeline: 988

- SAMHSA's National Helpline: 1-800-662-4357

- The Trevor Project: 1-866-488-7386

- Veterans Crisis Line: 988, then press 1

When you call a crisis line, you will be asked to give your permission to talk with a trained volunteer or the operator. They will provide you with information about what to expect from the service. You will have an opportunity to discuss what you are going through and your thoughts and feelings. The operator will stay on the line with you until you feel calmer and more stable. Many individuals wonder if their emotional state or situation is dire enough to call a crisis line. A good rule of thumb is to call if you are thinking of calling. When in doubt, reach out!

Consider Online Therapy Options

Technology has made online options for therapy more prevalent than ever. There are countless apps that allow you to send written and audio messages to your therapist whenever you need to vent or discuss an issue. These apps often have video-call features as well. Many of these are subscription services where you pay a monthly or annual fee. One thing to remember with online therapy is that your experience will only be as good as the therapist with whom you are matched. You may need to switch therapists several times before finding a good fit. You will also want to evaluate an online therapy option the same as you would a therapy app (which we'll discuss further later in this chapter).

Revisit Your Budget

This isn't an option available for everyone, but consider whether you can make some adjustments to your budget. Are there expenses you might be able to cut, even for the short term, to afford therapy? We often spend money on things we think will make us feel better, such as alcohol, takeout food, impulse purchases, fancy fitness gear, vacations, and manicures and pedicures. But these strategies only provide a short-term fix while depleting our wallets. Therapy can help you manage your stress and discover new coping methods that don't involve spending money.

Other Activities to Promote Mental Health

If therapy isn't accessible to you right now, other outlets can be beneficial. Any activity will benefit your mental health if it decreases isolation, promotes physical movement, helps you develop confidence, gives you a creative outlet, allows you to focus your attention on the present moment, or brings you a sense of fun or meaning. But be true to yourself and find an activity you genuinely like. If you hate reading, joining a book club is not for you. If you aren't into sports, don't make yourself play pickleball.

Join a Self-Help Book Club

Reading books on mental health can be a great way to prompt self-reflection and learn new coping skills. Gather any friends who are interested in self-care, mental wellness, or self-reflection and see if they might be open to meeting on a regular basis to discuss books on these topics. A book club can provide you with connection and support from others, along with the knowledge you gain from reading. It's also an excuse to make fancy appetizers for your friends. And who doesn't need a good excuse for snacks? Go ahead and get that wedge of brie and spinach dip from Trader Joe's. Puff pastry canapés for everyone!

The book you are currently holding in your hand (or listening to through your headphones) could be an excellent option to get your group started, but I'll admit to being a little biased. Here are a few other fantastic titles to consider:

- *Set Boundaries, Find Peace: A Guide to Reclaiming Yourself* by Nedra Glover Tawwab

- *The Happiness Trap: How to Stop Struggling and Start Living* by Russ Harris

- *Burnout: The Secret to Unlocking the Stress Cycle* by Emily Nagoski and Amelia Nagoski

- *Maybe You Should Talk to Someone: A Therapist,* Her *Therapist, and Our Lives Revealed* by Lori Gottlieb

- *Emotional First Aid: Healing Rejection, Guilt, Failure, and Other Everyday Hurts* by Guy Winch

- *You Can Heal Your Heart: Finding Peace After a Breakup, Divorce, or Death* by Louise Hay and David Kessler

- *The Shadow Work Workbook: Self-Care Exercises for Healing Your Trauma and Exploring Your Hidden Self* by Jor-El Caraballo

- *Feeling Great: The Revolutionary New Treatment for Depression and Anxiety* by David D. Burns

- *The Gifts of Imperfection: Let Go of Who You Think You're Supposed to Be and Embrace Who You Are* by Brené Brown

Try Out Improv Acting

Improvisational acting is a type of performance art where participants make up stories and scenes, typically comedy, on the spot. Improv classes are a great place to laugh and have fun, though the benefits of improv acting extend well beyond the ability to be funny on a stage. Anyone who has done improv acting will tell you that their mental health is better for it. Improv lets you try on different personas and explore new ways of being in the world. It gives you the freedom to make mistakes and practice radical acceptance, increasing your level of confidence and self-acceptance. Improv acting can also teach you important life skills, even if you have no intention of becoming a performer. These skills include:

- The ability to cope with changing circumstances

- Increased focus and attention

- The ability to develop rapport and work with others

- Enhanced perspective taking

- Better listening skills

- Increased emotional intelligence

- The ability to think in new and creative ways

- Improved leadership skills

- Greater ease of speaking in public

Look into Other Creative Outlets

Find a group environment where you can be accepted for who you are—no strings attached. That could be a dance troupe, gardening club, musical group, volunteer organization, or photography class. These creative outlets give you a sense of belonging, help you find meaning in life, and give you a chance to be in that transcendent flow state. I watched the Gay Men's Chorus of Washington, DC, and the GenOUT Youth Chorus perform last night. I was awestruck by their musical talent, and it was an honor to be in the presence of a group promoting diversity, equality, justice, and inclusion. Keep searching until you find your people.

Join a Sports Team

Many of my clients derive meaning from being part of a sports team, whether that be a recreational soccer or kickball league, a frisbee club, or a local softball team. They enjoy getting the opportunity to get physically active and meet new people. After the game, the group typically heads to dinner or happy hour. Having a space to connect with others that also adds structure to your week goes a long way in managing your mental health.

Use Mental Health Apps

Being on our phones usually gets a bad rap. Still, some excellent mental health apps exist. These apps have been created for everything under the sun, whether you're looking for simple guided mindfulness and meditation scripts, or want help with managing your anxiety and OCD. There are apps that help you track your self-care habits, monitor your mood and emotions, and provide journal prompts. Some great options include Calm, Happify, Headspace, PTSD Coach, the Mindfulness App, and Insight Timer.

When evaluating an app for your mental health, keep the following recommendations in mind:

1. Research the app to determine who developed it, where the developers got their funding, and whether they have any conflicts of interest. For example, you wouldn't want to purchase a healthy eating app sponsored by a candy bar company or fast-food conglomerate.

2. Look for any hidden costs or fees to avoid getting caught off guard. In the past, I've been excited to download a new "free" app only to find out that I must pay $12.99 a month after the trial period to access the fun and relevant content. Sometimes, I am okay with paying the monthly fee. Other times, I would rather spend that money on supporting my shoe-buying habit. New platforms for spring? Yes, please!

3. Consider your privacy and security as you share personal health information. Look into how the app uses and protects your data. Your health information is protected by federal law under the Health Insurance Portability and Accountability Act of 1996 (HIPAA). Under HIPAA, you have a right to know how your personal health information will be protected and used.

If the app doesn't clearly state how your information will be safeguarded, that might be a sign to consider other options.

4. Investigate if the app is based on clinical research and evidence-based interventions. You want to make sure that it has some solid science behind it. It can't just look cute.

5. Ask yourself if this app is something you will use regularly. This is especially important if you pay your hard-earned dollars for the service. Brain change requires small, consistent actions over time. In other words, I would rather you meditate for 5 minutes daily than for 45 minutes once a month. If you can't easily incorporate the app into your life, do yourself a favor and skip the download.

6. Determine if you can share the data collected through this app with your health providers. For example, if the app measures your level of anxiety or tracks your mood over time, can you print or download that graph to share with your psychiatrist or therapist?

Deciding if Medication Is Right for You

I have clients who are incredibly engaged in therapy. They make great strides toward changing how they respond to negative thoughts. They establish healthy boundaries in their lives. They incorporate healthy lifestyle changes like prioritizing quality sleep, physical activity, and meditation. But some of these clients still don't see the progress in their mental health that they would like to see, even though they are working incredibly hard. At this point, I will likely bring up the idea of adding medication as an additional tool to manage mental health. I will suggest that these clients talk to their primary care doctor, a psychiatrist, or a psychiatric nurse practitioner to be screened for psychotropic medication.

Medication is rarely a cure-all for mental health concerns. Still, it can be essential to a person's overall mental wellness plan. A prescription can give you greater capacity to make changes and create positive momentum in your life. One of my clients, Sonya, was a mom of two young kids. She experienced mild depression most of her life, first noticing symptoms in eighth grade, but was able to manage her symptoms with exercise and creative outlets like drawing and painting. Then life got increasingly busy for Sonya as she started a new job. Between work, a lack of reliable childcare, and no time to be alone, she felt like she was on a hamster wheel, unable to find any enjoyment in life. Sonya would go to bed at 8:30 p.m., wake up at 6:30 a.m., and still not feel rested. She spoke with a psychiatrist and started taking a low dose of an antidepressant, which helped her have more energy and made it much easier to manage her depression symptoms.

Unfortunately, there is still a stigma surrounding psychotropic medication. Many of us believe that we should be able to tackle mental health symptoms on our own. But if you had diabetes, you wouldn't try to manage it solely with lifestyle and behavioral changes. You would take insulin too. If you sprained your ankle, you wouldn't try to shake it off, get tough, or think positively. You would likely take pain medication along with ice, rest, and elevation. Mental health conditions aren't any different from physical conditions in this aspect. You can give yourself all the tools necessary to feel better.

For a long time, I resisted taking medication to manage depression symptoms. Like many, I believed I could manage with exercise, positive thinking, and more organization. Those things are essential for me, and they do help. But when I am not on medication, I have a more challenging time being myself. I'm prone to ruminate over negative events. I have much less energy—not even Lizzo's songs can pump me up. And I *really* love Lizzo. My plants start to die because I'm too tired to water them. Starting and finishing projects is tough. Simple tasks, like scheduling eye appointments and going through my mail, feel overwhelming. I am a cranky and less fun person to be around, making me more reluctant to make plans with friends so I can shield them from my swamp-witch funk. Medication isn't a magic wand, but it gives me more bandwidth to do the things that make me feel like me.

Like all medications, there can be side effects to psychotropic prescriptions. Depending on the medication you take, these side effects can include fatigue, weight changes, difficulty sleeping, dry mouth, constipation, and sexual complications. Discuss the pros and cons of starting medication with your prescriber. You can also talk about strategies to manage side effects with your therapist.

Now What?

Now that you have this newfound information on strategies to improve your mental health, you may be asking yourself, *What do I do now?* You might be feeling overwhelmed and wondering where to start. There is no right or wrong way to begin. Pick one small action that speaks to you and put your focus there. If the section on challenging your inner critic spoke to you, start paying more attention to your negative thoughts and see if you can challenge or reframe your thinking. If the information on the mind-body connection piqued your interest, try out a few methods for regulating your nervous system, like meditation or grounding techniques. See if you can implement a new strategy for self-care this week, like not checking email or other messages until after you drink your coffee and eat breakfast. One positive change will lead to another, and you will build momentum from there.

I'm Rooting for You

My clients come to therapy because they're concerned that they are too anxious or down and should be happier or more energetic. But the truth is, most of my clients are reacting normally to an abnormal (dare

I say, fucked up?) world. They are not broken, flawed, or lazy. Neither are you.

Intense and overwhelming emotions are a natural reaction to the constant threat of gun violence, worldwide pandemics, climate change, discrimination, racial and political tensions, financial instability, attacks on bodily autonomy, and the erosion of human rights. Not to mention the constant pressure to succeed in today's hustle culture. We receive nearly constant updates on these calamities and societal expectations thanks to modern technology. Unlike our prehistoric ancestors, these dangers can't be outrun. It's a lot for our human brains and nervous systems to manage. Most of us are doing surprisingly well given the circumstances.

Your task is to figure out how to function in this abnormal world. You must protect yourself from becoming overwhelmed by the pressures of modern life. You have to safeguard your energy and mental clarity to maintain compassion and advocate for a better future. Nothing will change if you are shut down, numbed out, exhausted, and out of touch with your values.

I can't change the fact that life can be painful and challenging. That's part of being human. But you can ease your suffering by refining your self-care activities, challenging your unhelpful thoughts, managing your emotions, investing in relationships, setting healthy boundaries, and creating meaning in your life. You can care for your friends, family, communities, country, and world by loving and healing yourself first.

As this book comes to a close, Nelson, naturally, would like to get in a few words and speak on behalf of all the other inner critics out there:

LIZ: Okay, Nelson, whatcha got to say?

NELSON: Listen, as your inner critic, I get that I can be harsh sometimes.

LIZ: That would be an understatement.

NELSON: I'm not trying to be evil, scary, or a jerk.

LIZ: I know.

NELSON: All the other inner critics out there and I are just trying to protect you and others from getting hurt, embarrassed, or rejected. We actually aren't all that powerful. We just get anxious and afraid.

LIZ: Thanks for saying that. I know you are just trying to look out for me, Nelson, but you don't have to work so hard. I love you, buddy. We got this.

NELSON: I know. I love you too.

Give yourself a ton of credit for taking the time to read this book and reflect on your mental health. It would have been easier to scroll through social media, drink beer, and go with the grind of daily life, but you decided you want more. You've come to the conclusion that you are worthy of feeling better—that you want to intentionally live your life with purpose. That's a big deal, and I am rooting for you.

Action Items

1. What feels like a logical next step, big or small, to improve your mental wellness?

2. Could you use some additional support in your life? What would that support look like? How could you reach out for support from your friends, family, or community?

3. What are the top three things you will take away from reading this?

ENDNOTES

1   ASD Market Week. (2022, January 11). *What self-care trends means for retailers in 2023.* https://asdonline.com/blog/retail-news/what-self-care-trends-mean-for -retailers-in-2020

2   World Economic Forum. (2021, April 21). *Feeling good: The future of the $1.5 trillion wellness market.* https://www.weforum.org/agenda/2021/04/wellness -market-mental-health-physical-mckinsey-consumers-retail-lifestyle/

3   Nagoski, E., & Nagoski, A. (2019). *Burnout: The secret to unlocking the stress cycle.* Ballantine Books, p. 15.

4   Anderson, F. G. (2021). *Transcending trauma: Healing complex PTSD with internal family systems therapy.* PESI Publishing, p. xvii.

5   Cuddy, A. (2012, October). *Your body language may shape who you are* [Video]. TED Conferences. https://www.ted.com/talks/amy_cuddy_your_body_language _may_shape_who_you_are/comments

6   Largo-Wight, E., Wlyudka, P. S., Merten, J. W., & Cuvelier, E. A. (2017). Effectiveness and feasibility of a 10-minute employee stress intervention: Outdoor booster break. *Journal of Workplace Behavioral Health, 32*(3), 159–171. https://doi .org/10.1080/15555240.2017.1335211

7   Neuroscience News. (2016, June 15). *Making art reduces stress hormones.* https://neurosciencenews.com/cortisol-art-stress-4480/

8   National Institutes of Health. (2019). *Practicing gratitude: Ways to improve positivity.* NIH News in Health. https://newsinhealth.nih.gov/2019/03 /practicing-gratitude

9   Eron, K., Kohnert, L., Watters, A., Logan, C., Weisner-Rose, M., & Mehler, P. S. (2020). Weighted blanket use: A systematic review. *American Journal of Occupational Therapy, 74*(2), 7402205010p1–7402205010p14. https://doi .org/10.5014/ajot.2020.037358

10 White, A. (2022). *Not drinking tonight: A guide to creating a sober life you love.* Hachette Go.

11 Brown, B. (2019, May 31). *What being sober has meant to me.* https://brenebrown .com/articles/2019/05/31/what-being-sober-has-meant-to-me/

12 Zahrai, S. (2020, December 14). *Inspower series ep. 14 | 6 steps to emotional self-regulation—overcoming amygdala hijack* [Video]. Shadé Zahrai. https://www .shadezahrai.com/post/inspower-series-ep-14-6-steps-to-emotional-self-regulation -overcoming-amygdala-hijack

13   TED. (2017, April 12). *Sarah Knight: The magic of not giving a f**** [Video]. YouTube. https://www.youtube.com/watch?v=GwRzjFQa_Og

14   Brown, B. (2018, October 15). *Clear is kind. Unclear is unkind.* https://brenebrown.com/articles/2018/10/15/clear-is-kind-unclear-is-unkind/

15   Garis, M. G. (2020, January 30). *The Gottman Institute says there are 5 components of trust—and only 1 is honesty.* Well+Good. https://www.wellandgood.com/someone-you-cant-trust/

16   TED. (2008, July 15). *Helen Fisher: The brain in love* [Video]. YouTube. https://www.youtube.com/watch?v=OYfoGTIG7pY

17   Devine, M. (2018, March 9). *Pain vs suffering: You can't solve grief, but you don't have to suffer.* Refuge in Grief. https://refugeingrief.com/?p=5481

18   TED. (2019, April 25). *Nora McInerny: We don't "move on" from grief. We move forward with it* [Video]. YouTube. https://www.youtube.com/watch?v=khkJkR-ipfw

19   Tonkin, L. (1996). Growing around grief—another way of looking at grief and recovery. *Bereavement Care, 15*(1), 10. https://doi.org/10.1080/02682629608657376

20   Kaufman, S. B. (2016, January 30). *The differences between happiness and meaning in life.* Scientific American Blog Network. https://blogs.scientificamerican.com/beautiful-minds/the-differences-between-happiness-and-meaning-in-life/

21   TED. (2017, September 26). *Emily Esfahani Smith: There's more to life than being happy* [Video]. YouTube. https://www.youtube.com/watch?v=y9Trdafp83U

22   Brown, B. (2022). *The gifts of imperfection: Let go of who you think you're supposed to be and embrace who you are* (10th ed.). Hazelden Publishing, p. 35.

23   Rubin, G. (2011, July 15). *I don't have to chase extraordinary moments to find happiness—it's right in front of me: An interview with Brené Brown.* Forbes. https://www.forbes.com/sites/gretchenrubin/2011/07/15/i-dont-have-to-chase-extraordinary-moments-to-find-hapiness-its-right-in-front-of-me/

24   Kim, R. (2022, March 7). *Addressing the lack of diversity in the mental health field.* NAMI. https://nami.org/Blogs/NAMI-Blog/March-2022/Addressing-the-Lack-of-Diversity-in-the-Mental-Health-Field

25   J. Caraballo (personal communication, April 2, 2023)

ACKNOWLEDGMENTS

It takes a village to write a book. I am so lucky to have some wonderful people in my corner. I am incredibly thankful to the team at Bridge City Books and PESI Publishing, especially Kayla Church and Karsyn Morse, for taking a chance on me. I am also so fortunate to have had the incomparable Jenessa Jackson as an editor and Emily Dyer as a designer. Thank you, Jenessa and Emily, for making this book better than I ever could have imagined! The entire group at PESI is not only good at what they do, but they are also some of the nicest people I've ever met.

To all the outstanding speakers I listened to and met with at the Psychotherapy Networker Symposium in Washington, DC, thank you for sharing your knowledge with the world and providing me with powerful inspiration.

Dr. Christopher Willard and Dr. Mitch Abblett, this book wouldn't have been possible without your instruction, guidance, and enthusiasm. Taking your workshop sparked this entire project.

Thank you, Dr. William Kirk, for being so supportive and for helping me navigate my career change to the mental health field. You are a shining light to me and to many!

Tom Mauch, your top-notch advice, perspective, and friendship are so appreciated. (I owe you tacos and drinks.)

Trish Gomersall, thank you for being one of my first readers and for your stellar editing skills. Adara Mitchell, you are the queen of web design and a delightful person to work with.

Lynn Grodski, you made me believe I could be a writer and helped me figure out how to make writing possible. I am grateful to have you as a coach!

To the staff at the Wendt Center for Loss and Healing, particularly Stephanie Handel, Grace Metz, Susan Greynolds, and Michelle Palmer,

I have learned so much from you. Thank you for helping me get my start in social work and mental health. You are a stellar organization, and I am in awe of your work.

To Elizabeth Hinkle and Dustin Winkel, you are the best peer-supervision group anyone could ask for. Thank you for giving me a safe place to talk when I feel stuck and for your unconditional support. I am also hugely grateful to my therapist colleagues who are only a text, email, or postcard away, particularly Sharon Greenbaum, Amy Cirbus, Kate Rosenblatt, Meaghan Rice, Ashley Ertel, Jor-El Caraballo, Lisa Kays, Cynthia Catchings, Bobbie Merlino, and Jill Daino.

Alison Tygiel, I love you. Thank you for teaching me to swear, order sushi, and not care what other people think. I appreciate you for always being my hype girl!

Suhail Khan, thank you for being one of my first friends in Washington, DC, and for always being there for me. You two make me laugh harder than anyone else I know.

To Judson Richardson and Carol Bartlett, thank you for being my first social work mentors. I am so grateful the universe brought us together. I am lucky to have you as friends. Your excellent clinical judgment and wisdom, commitment to ethics, wicked sense of humor, and impromptu dance parties have saved me more times than I can count.

Thank you to my incredible mom, Katherine Kelly, for being a trailblazer and showing me that I can do big things, and to my brother, Michael Kelly, who brings out my smart-ass side and confidence. I love you both!

Finally, thank you to my smart, enthusiastic, and supportive husband, JonMarc Buffa. Thank you for believing in me and picking up the slack with our sweet kids while I was frantically typing away at my computer. I love you!

ABOUT THE AUTHOR

 Liz Kelly, LICSW, is a psychotherapist, clinical social worker, and writer living in Northern Virginia outside Washington, DC. She specializes in helping busy people create meaning, reduce stress, and live more intentionally. Liz also works with individuals contending with grief, loss, and other life transitions. Outside of work, she goes on weekend adventures with her husband and two daughters. She loves getting creative and organized (if she weren't a therapist, she would organize closets for a living!), trying new recipes, watching random documentary films, hiking, and hanging out with her friends and neighbors.